Plant & Roots

A social history of Ballater before the Beatles and Dr. Beeching

by

Ian Cameron

D1470712

Dedicated to Margaret

Published in 2008 by
Pica Design
51 Charlton Crescent,
Aboyne, Aberdeenshire
AB34 5GN

Many thanks to Hugh Stewart for his help and advice
during the preparation of this book.

Most photographs reproduced in this book were either taken by the author,
or were part of a collection of images left to him by his late friend Mike
Sheridan. Others have been collected over the years and their sources are
now unknown - the author hopes he may be forgiven if copyright has
been unintentionally infringed.

ISBN 978-0-9561126-0-6

Typesetting by Harry Scott (Pica Design, Aboyne)
Printed and bound by F. Crowe & Son Ltd.
Distributed by Deeside Books, 18-20 Bridge Street, Ballater, AB35 5QP.
Tel/Fax: 013397 54080. Email: deesidebk@aol.com

Introduction

Plant (mechanical) and roots (ancestral and sylvan) play a major part in this tale, which takes the young Cameron from his first sighting of, to his first wearing of khaki. Hitler's War clad countless thousands in that colour and moved men in millions, worldwide. One minor migration made of my boyhood world a new-found land for Newfoundlanders. That world was the environs of Ballater, never a Royal burgh but uniquely the burgh for Royalty in Scotland, as its numerous Warrants testify. Recollections of its transformation, after the transatlantic influx, are among the earlier memories of this memoir. Hitler's War cut down in their prime men in multitudes and trees in millions. The Newfoundlanders' deforestation in defence of the realms, ours at first and ultimately theirs, is another theme. Hitler's War of rapid movement pitched machines, as well as men, against each other in a manner unimaginable by the great generals of the past. The mechanical revolution it started and continued was mainly martial, but had a civilian element, not least in the logistics of logging. The Newfoundlanders swung axes against the Axis, and the axe was a Stone Age concept. They still sweated over saws, single and two-man, as their ancestors had done: the saw had started cutting in the Bronze Age. Widespread use then in Britain of that German invention, Andreas Stihl's chain-saw, was of course denied them. The transport of trees, however, saw the slow start of a mechanisation that has resulted over six decades in logging leviathans which make light of heavy loads in inaccessible places. The boy Cameron saw and the man participated in and oversaw that transformation. Hitler's War created heavy hardships which did not end with cessation of hostilities. Most of its succeeding decade was an age of austerity, as, in my world, had been that which preceded it. That entire period saw the worthy have it hard where, many of its generation would say, the unworthy now have it easy. The hard years had a contrasting happiness also recorded in these remembrances. The man who wants to remember, ironically, shares a birthday with the regiment that recruits men who want to forget, France's Foreign Legion. It entered the world under Citizen King Louis-Philippe in 1831 and he under King George VI in 1938.

Chapter 1.

Memory holds the door

The childhood shows the man, As morning shows the day:
John Milton: Paradise Regained

I was born at 6am on Wednesday the 9th of March 1938. The house in which I was delivered by our late doctor, Sir George Middleton, is still there in Albert Road, Ballater. I lived in that house until I reluctantly left for National Service in February 1960.

On my return, two years later, Margaret and I married and we left for Dunkeld and a busy eight years with the Forestry Commission.

Force of circumstance saw us back in Aberdeen in 1970. There I spent two years as a mature student, catching up on new Maths and English, skills much in demand as James and Jennifer started to come to me with homework.

The next year was spent setting up a training facility for motor apprentices. I then moved on to Alexander Hall (Builders) in Aberdeen as assistant plant manager. Five hectic years followed: the whole world was changing with North Sea oil. I left to set up Castle Plant (Deeside) Ltd., which has occupied my life ever since.

In 1975, we moved to a house that we had built at Kintore, and ten years later moved to Kincardine O'Neil, where Margaret was housekeeper at Borrowstone House to Mrs. Maida Stephen of the Clydebank shipbuilding family. Their shipyard, Stephen of Linthouse, was noteworthy for building Amethyst, the ship that in April 1949 steamed down the Yangtse River running the gauntlet of Communist Chinese guns. Later, Stephen was the workplace of a Glasgow welder, one Billy Connolly. When Mrs Stephen died, we moved to Abergairn, Ballater. That was the same Abergairn, home of three generations of Grants in the 1800s, where John Grant wrote 'The Legends of the Braes o' Mar.'

We attended a local concert in the Albert Hall soon after returning to Ballater. Sitting there among 'kent faces', I suddenly saw my Book, content and theme.

It was complete in my mind before the concert finished. Pressures of Castle Plant work, and, in the past six years, time spent on Community Council wrangles, have delayed the writing. Now I feel Book One is almost complete.

The Ballater I write of is the Ballater of my childhood memories, a Ballater that had grown organically through the 1800s from its original planned town grid to a railway terminus, a part-year garrison town and then a major tourist destination from which to tour Deeside.

All that growth came to a sudden end with World War I. The Ballater into which I was born in 1938 was stuck in a 1914 time warp. Apart from the picture house and two blocks of the very first council houses in Scotland, nothing had been built in the village since the outbreak of the Great War.

By the end of World War II, the town had suffered a further five years of overcrowding and neglect that the remains of military camps, stables and two very ruined mansions showed.

The village still boasted numerous joinery workshops; there, in their Edwardian heyday, the pitch-pine and oak doors, staircases and windows of the great villas yet to be seen in Braemar and Queens Roads had been made. There were masons' open-fronted sheds, slaters' dressing sheds, old stables with hay lofts, coal yards with heaps of war-strategic coal that had never been issued; and old garages full of cars laid up in 1939 that were never to run again. There were flocks of sheep on the golf course and coops of hens in a field beside the engine sheds not 70 yards from the Station Square.

That Ballater has gone for ever. We have marched on, but that is the Ballater I write of, not researched from academic records or heard of second-hand, but seen, listened to and smelt as a child discovering my world with a pleasure and the curiosity that drives me still.

Of course, at that age I did not understand the reasons and interpretation I can now attach to events, nor character that I bestow on my individuals. That comes only with the experiences of life, encounters, and the revelations of time. On my various forays into the realms of local history and legend, I can truly claim the first-hand source of these tales to be my grandmother.

Agnes Mary Cameron was born at the Milton, close by the Milton Burn in Gairnside. She went to school at Kirkstyle, next to the church and just round the corner from Gairnshiel Bridge. 'Dolly' as she was known, loved Glen Gairn and she revelled in its history.

Her father, James Cameron, was county roadman responsible for the Gairnside road from its junction with the Ballater-Braemar road at Foot of Gairn right up to Gairnshiel Bridge, that at a time of gravel surfaces, but very few cars. He was also responsible for two fords, one beneath Amy Fraser's Manse (see her 'Hills of Home') and another at Candacraig on the old road to Morven.

James Cameron was a contemporary of the Grants of the 'Legends of the Braes o' Mar' fame, and I have no reason to disbelieve that the forenicht tales at one peat fire would be any different from another in a close-knit community like Gairnside.

The fairy hillocks, the *Sidheanan* of Gaelic, abound in Upper Deeside, and the little people often cropped up in my grandmother's stories.

What brought an awesome realisation of the power of primitive forces was my grandmother's firm belief that an old lady who lived alone at Stronley was a witch. Twice a year, she ran round her thatched cottage carrying a three-legged pot in which a peat fire burned. My grandmother and her brothers and sisters all witnessed that ritual, and could tell me that it took place on the first day of May and again on the first day of November, and they insisted that the old witch ran with the sun, clockwise, round her house. Many years later, I happened to be at the Standing Stones of Callanish in Lewis on Mid-summer's day 1984. There I watched a German woman dance with the sun round the great stones. She, interestingly enough, used an old Gaelic-English term 'deiseal-wise' to describe her path from east to south to west around the circle.

In the course of its 30-year existence, Castle Plant has owned many excavators and dug many holes. In my Forestry Commission days, I was involved in the construction of forest roads throughout Perthshire and Fife and I soon came to understand that there is no such thing as an ordinary stone, only an infinite variety of mineral and rock types. That insatiable curiosity led me to study geology and this in turn opened up a whole new world. Suddenly landscapes took on a new perspective. Where, up till then, I had sought out woods and relict groups of old Caledonian Umbrella Pines, I would now search out old mines, fault lines and sources of agates and cairngorms. The pleasure of living here at Abergairn is all the more intense with the lead mines at our back door.

Years of experience digging holes led to an ability to read the ground. That meant that one could predict if, for example, this unnaturally level, round area of ground was the site of a 4000-year-old Bronze Age hut circle or just a gun emplacement from World War II manoeuvres. One could distinguish between an old General Wade military road from 1725 and a grouse-moor access road from the 1960s. General Wade's road was invariably better engineered.

At a time of light snow cover or in the summer evenings with low sun and long shadows, or even on the moors that first autumn after a severe heather burn, the earth speaks to you and reveals shapes and forms of old mineral workings, ruins, lime kilns, clearance cairns, hut circles and long-forgotten animal enclosures. It is so tantalising and yet intense, you can almost hear the siren call: 'Here is your heritage, here is your past.'

Now that I have revealed my sources, enjoy the book.

Chapter 2.

Rose, rowan and remembrance

Glen Gairn... *from Gleann Gharain, glen of the crying one, referring to the stream:*
Adam Watson and Elizabeth Allan:
The Place Names of Upper Deeside

A mile west of Ballater, the A93 road is joined by the A939. That is the road that leads up Glen Gairn and over the hills to Speyside. Three miles up Glen Gairn, the road crosses the Milton Burn by a narrow bridge; downstream this burn soon joins the River Gairn, but above the road, earthworks on its east bank reveal where the mill had stood harnessing the tumbling waters to grind corn. On the opposite bank can still be seen the ruined walls of a cottage, the vigilant rowan and a very, very wild rose bush. A dyke still encloses the kale yard, the rich soil feeding sheep where once it supported our family. That was the Milton, the thatched cottage of James Cameron, road man of Glen Gairn, and birthplace of my grandmother, Agnes (Dolly) Cameron.

Ruins of the Milton Cottage

Dolly would joke of being the last child born at the Milton before the roof fell in, but that was her way of coping with memories of abject poverty and watching her mother's struggle with always another bairn. The family's heartbreak at losing twins at a month old after a bitterly severe January in the clay-floored, draughty, damp cottage led the Camerons to move down the glen to Ballachrosk, nearer Ballater. My great-grandparents were casualties of Invercauld Estate's policies of clearing their ground of small tenants by refusing to maintain their thatched cottages while still charging rent for the ruin.

Dolly started school at Ballater from Ballachrosk. In later life she would tell how reluctant she was to leave Ballater School and finish her education at Kirkstyle when the family moved back up the glen to Dalfad.

When pressed as to why the family made that move when the general tendency then was to 'move down to Ballater,' Dolly explained that her father's work was still in the glen. Also Dalfad, unlike the previous houses, had a little bit of ground where they kept sheep, goats and hens and could grow potatoes and corn.

More cynically, she said: 'We just crossed the water'.

What she left unsaid was that the 'water' was the River Gairn, and the Gairn was the march or boundary between two great estates, Invercauld on the South and Morven on the North. By moving across the Gairn to Dalfad, they were let a much better house, set up to the sun, near the minister's family at the manse and owned by Keiller of Dundee, whose new marmalade money had bought the Morven estate from the Marquis of Huntly.

The Camerons were to stay at Dalfad till after the Great War.

The family was happy there. In later years, Dalfad days were always recalled as endless summers, helping with hay, gathering blaeberries and cranberries on the hills, catching rabbits in the stone dykes, and meeting Stalker's horse-drawn grocer cart at the ford on the Gairn at the foot of the Manse Brae.

They lived in an enchanted world. The children found and played in fairy circles, only now being recognised as Bronze Age hut circles: clearance cairns above the fields became castles, and the stone walls of ancient cattle folds draped the hill sides above them like necklaces.

People had lived and farmed the lime-rich glen continuously since the last Ice Age. They were a free folk: a fish from the river, a beast from the hill and a tree from the wood were necessities for survival and a right that was not abused.

Gairnshiel cattle fold

The changes came after Culloden.

Beneath Dalfad, the McGregors had mustered on the haugh by the Gairn before marching off to follow Charlie. The six survivors of the 24 that marched on to Culloden Moor returned to find a new order.

The network of military road-building that was initiated after the 1715 rising had crossed the Gairn with a high-arched bridge at Gairnshiel, one of many on a new road that ran from Stirling Castle to Fort George on the Moray Firth. Whole regiments garrisoned the Highlands, with roads and security both vastly improved. The old Clan system collapsed and gradually the Eastern Highland Clearances made way for the creation of deer forests, grouse moors and *sport*.

Sport brought unlikely neighbours. At the end of the Crimean War, Lord Cardigan took the lease of Corndavon Lodge. That was the same Lord Cardigan who had given his title to the heavy woollen sweater he wore in the Crimea. The same Lord Cardigan had bought his commission in the British Army and in the space of two years made seven hundred arrests and held one hundred and five courts-martial within his regiment of only three hundred and fifty men. The very same Lord Cardigan rode at the head of the Charge of the Light Brigade on 25th October 1854, and later that night dined on his own steam yacht anchored off Sebastopol.

Living sustainably with nature was then interpreted as poaching, a serious crime. Time would prove how unsustainable the commercial *sport* of grouse shooting and salmon fishing would be.

Be that as it may, James Cameron with six of a family to feed risked job, house and Sheriff by shooting hare, deer, and partridge, and with net and gaff caught trout and salmon in the Gairn. Dolly used to tell of frosty, moonlit nights when her father would dispatch the boys to drive the woods and she would be taken with him to the old Catholic chapel in Dalfad birch wood to wait crouched behind the ruined wall for the deer.

Gairnshiel Military Bridge

Dalfad ruined chapel

Dolly's job was to carry a bag with the powder, wads and lead bullets to reload the then fifty-year old muzzle-loading rifle. She used to recall the fatal night that her father shot a red setter belonging to a neighbouring farmer in mistake for a roe deer. She used to describe how the gun was laboriously reloaded. Black powder was poured down the barrel from a flask, a wad of paper rammed down, more powder, paper, powder, paper. Finally came ramming of the heavy lead ball, melted down from an old water pipe. Only then could the hunt restart.

Gairnside school pupils

She used to recall Gairnside School, Church, Christmas time and parties, parties at the manse and parties at the Keiller lairds' sandstone mansion house on Craigendarroch. Dolly used to tell of leaving the warmth of the Keiller party in cold mid-winter nights and coming home the long five miles in the back of a horse-drawn farm cart, cuddled together with her school friends under the stars, and protected from the Glen Gairn winter only by sheaves of straw.

The Clan culture of discipline and family had vanished. The glens, teeming with wildlife, brought the *sportsmen* and the slaughter. The earliest shooting lodges were built right in the hills, Callater, Cluny, Corndavon and Morven, and it was the Morven Estate, complete with Lodge, that 'auld Keiller' bought from the Marquis of Huntly.

The new Lairds of Morven. To my grandmother there were the two Keillers: 'Auld Keiller' was John Mitchell Keiller, who had gained control of the family business in 1877 on his father's death and in 1883 married Mary Sime Greig of the noted Dundee medical family. By1885, he had made his purchase.

J.M.Keiller had always suffered from ill health and commissioned his Dundee architects to build a mansion for him just out of Ballater on his own estate so as to be convenient for the train and to avoid the long coach drive up to Morven Lodge. Because his architects' building medium was sandstone, that house was built of pink sandstone from Fife quarries, each dressed stone being transported by train to Ballater. So now we have forever the anomaly of a sandstone house on a granite hill. The locals called it 'the marmalade house' alluding to both colour and capital. Several owners, and one hundred years on, it is the Hilton Craigendarroch of today.

John Mitchell Keiller retired from active management of James Keiller & Sons Ltd. in 1893, moving to his new house in Hyde Park Gardens, London, only to die at sea in his steam-yacht, Erl King ,while cruising in the West Indies on 2nd January 1899.

'Young Keiller' or Alexander Keiller, is remembered locally as flying the first aircraft ever seen on Deeside and for having a garage of vehicles varying from Bugatti racing cars to Citroen Kegresse half-tracks. The Bugattis used to race the Deeside trains and the Citroen went on archaeological digs to the top of Morven hill and the Coyles of Muick.

He carries the blame for the run down of the estate, but we must remember that the Great War left the whole country in ruin, and then World War II came along.

Alexander Keiller's great passion was amateur archaeology. By 1920, the family firm had been bought by Crosse & Blackwell and he was able to follow his hobby full-time. He succeeded in sinking his fortune in digging holes at Avebury, which today is acknowledged as a great work.

Alex Keiller married four times: his last wife and widow, Gabrielle, left his museum at Avebury to the nation. Avebury was declared a World Heritage Site in 1986 and in 2000 it received 350,000 visitors. The ashes of Alexander and Gabrielle Keiller are buried at Abergairn Castle.

Various members of the Keiller/Greig dynasty came to Deeside to build villas. Some were welcome: other cousins were refused building ground on the estate. At that rebuff, they promptly petitioned Invercauld for ground as near to the Morven estate as possible at Clashinruich, close to the old Catholic chapel, high in the Glen Gairn hills. There they started construction, quarrying into the Mammie Hill above for building stone.

An old track cut off from the Military Road to pass Clashinruich Chapel and carry on skirting Dalfad and a row of one-park crofts till it reached the Ardoch, then a substantial farm, but originally a Roman Catholic settlement. One of the masons at the building of Clashinruich was Charlie Cumming and along

Citroen Kegresse half-tracks

the track to Ardoch Farm was Maggie Cumming's cottage and park. I have often wondered if they were related. Charlie Cumming went on to become burgh foreman in Ballater, responsible for the water supply and the reservoir at Foot of Gairn, responsible for graveyards, rubbish collection, annual pruning of Kirk green trees and clearing snow. After the picture house opened, Charlie Cumming became the feared custodian of order there, armed with a powerful torch and his battle cry of: 'Stop the Takking, Stop the Takking'.

The Great War interrupted the construction of Clashinruich, and indeed a way of life. All the young men were called up, many never to return.

In the words of a local conscript: 'At 6.10am, the artillery barrage started. At 6.16am, the battalion went across. As a matter of fact, our artillery barrage was absolutely feeble, and what there was of it fell on our own men. The Germans were out of their trenches firing at our men all the time the barrage was on and shouted out to our men: "Come on, don't funk it". 'Then, when our men did get up, half of them were so stiff with cold they staggered about. However, they all pushed on extraordinarily well. The Germans were shoulder to shoulder in front of their trench and also in it, firing rapid fire. Their trenches were also stiff with machine guns. Our men got about 50 yards and then, finding only two officers left and half the men gone, they knew they could go no further. Some of them got back at once to the trench we held; the remainder who were not wounded lay down in shell holes where they were.' 'All this happened in 8 minutes.'

After the war, Charlie Cumming and the builders returned and Clashinruich house was completed.

From this brief insight of my roots I move on to my first memories.

Clashinruich

Chapter 3.

Arms and the Man

Let who desires peace prepare for war [Flavius Vegetius Renatus]:
Justin Wintle:
The Dictionary of War Quotations:

In the early thirties, two saloon cars produced in separate factories in the industrial Midlands of England were bought by Ballater owners. One was a Morris 10, the other an Austin 10.

Both gave unremarkable but reliable service to their possessors, providing transport for Sunday outings, visits to church, weddings, funerals and annual holidays. The cars tended to be laid up all winter, drained of water and jacked up to take the weight off their tyres.

Everything changed with World War II.

The Morris was not laid up with the introduction of petrol rationing but fitted with a drawbar. Coupled to a small trailer, it was pressed into service with a builder, hauling sand, lime, tools and men on work deemed war-essential within the suddenly bustling district.

Nor was the Austin laid up with the onset of hostilities. A more radical fate was in store for the little vehicle. There was a need for a cart to deliver milk in bottles and cans from a newly-opened dairy set up to cater for the burgeoning camps of soldiers and Canadian lumberjacks. In the national interest, the rear of the Austin's body was hacked off and replaced with a wooden platform effectively converting the car into a light truck.

Everything was happening so fast. The seasonal holiday village that basked in Royal patronage and resultant tourist attention each August was thrown into the twentieth century and the reality of war.

This was high season and Highland Games time. Indeed, Wright's Amusements, the travelling show people, were already in the Games Park setting up their stalls. Roll-the-penny stalls were erected, swing boats, roundabouts for the

19

smaller children, shooting arcades for the men to flaunt their skills and a row of slot machines. The Wright family covered at least three generations, from the new babies up to Mr Wright senior, a patriarch figure, yet hardly tall enough to see over the bonnet of his huge American Hudson Terraplane car. This car, his pride and joy, was rendered instantly impotent by the out-break of war that brought fuel rationing, and authorities that steered family, caravans, trucks and amusements into a contractor's yard in Albert Road to sit out the hostilities. The Wright children became our little school friends.

Workmen appeared from everywhere. Stables were being built, simple structures of rough concrete bases with cast-in scaffold poles that carried asbestos roofs. Broken asbestos sheets were to be our lethal play things long after the war.

Pill boxes were built to cover Ballater Bridge and the road from Braemar. Hatches were built into the bridge to house explosives to destroy the structure should Germans get that close. All road signs were removed to confuse enemy paratroopers, but, as Lord Haw-Haw so chillingly broadcast; all the troops had to do was to visit the nearest graveyard to establish where they had landed.

Wartime stables

Ballater Home Guard

A detachment of the Home Guard was formed, commanded by the manager of the 'looms', the local tweed warehouse, selected for his military knowledge from the last war. Rifles were in very short supply and Home Guard parades saw men armed with an interesting selection of weaponry, from agricultural implements through antique muzzle-loading heirlooms to a variety of shotguns and deer-stalking rifles.

The local Territorial Army members had already been called up, as had the county council roadmen. The latter had become instant Royal Engineers and had departed for Biggin Hill Fighter Command Station complete with steam road-roller to repair bomb damage to the runways.

That mass exodus of local manpower was replaced by train load after train load of British Army units of infantry, artillery, engineers, commandos, and, strangest of all, Indian mountain artillerymen complete with mules and turbans.

Some of the soldiers were billeted in commandeered mansion houses, Monaltrie House and the old Glenmuick House. Others were quartered in Nissen huts and tented camps.

The hastily-erected stables were soon full of horses and mules. Endless strings of animals pulling rattling gun carriages were daily in training manoeuvres on the surrounding hills. Ballater was no stranger to the garrison role; it boasted its own barracks, built in the Victorian times, complete with Indian hill station verandas!

Ballater Barracks

The plans for the Royal Guard buildings had gone to the Raj by mistake, to be duly built on the north-west frontier, while local tradesmen struggled to construct India-intended buildings that would contend with the Deeside winters.

In peace time, the Victoria Barracks were occupied for only two months a year by the Highland regiment acting as Royal Guard to the Sovereign at Balmoral. Now it was packed with infantry, often the Gordon Highlanders, the local regiment, who had requisitioned a private house opposite the rear gate as the officers' mess and renamed it 'Bydand', the regimental motto. War-time parties there would become the stuff of local legend.

Chapter 4.

Blood and Iron

Blut und Eisen [Otto von Bismarck]:
>   The Oxford Dictionary of Quotations
>   Second Edition

War, total war as exemplified by Hitler's hostilities, became highly organised and mechanised: as such, it was deeply dependent on raw material. Churchill recognised at an early stage in the war that 'neutral' Sweden's great reserves of high-grade iron ore were central to Germany's war machine. It was to block the winter passage of ore through Norway when the Baltic was frozen over that British forces were sent to Narvik, early in 1940.

In a similar manner, the resources of Scotland's forests took on a strategic importance for the second time in one century. Ironically, most of the indigenous woodmen had been called up to serve in the Highland infantry regiments, and the shortfall in labour was taken up by Newfoundland and Canadian Forestry Corps men. The Newfoundlanders worked mainly with the lighter pit-props for the coal mines, another very strategic industry. The Canadians with their heavier machinery concentrated on railway sleepers and poles.

The very best logs went to build anti-tank obstacles for south coast beaches.

The Newfoundland Overseas Forestry Unit had many camps throughout the Highlands and was brought over primarily to cut pit props for British coalmines that were consuming the timber at the rate of 12,000 tons per day. Ultimately over 3500 men in 35 camps served in the Scottish woods. Newfoundland was a separate dominion during the war and did not join up with Canada until after a referendum in 1949. That explains why I talk of them individually.

Very rapidly sawmills were built, new 1940s technology, diesel-powered plants with many times the output of the traditional portable steam-engine powered, manual bench mills. Close to Ballater station, on its own siding, was built an all-electric mill. That was the 'Novellie' mill, built privately by Latvian Jews forced out of the Baltic timber trade by the Nazi movement. Those timber merchants had anticipated the emergency and had secured huge stocks of timber in Scotland.

Ballater Railway Station was central to all traffic movements in the valley; it was the terminus for Upper Deeside. In the early years of the war, trains ran night and day. Whole regiments and all their equipment moved in and out as intensive training gave way to action overseas. The Newfoundland and Canadian lumberjacks steamed in, separate goods trains bringing their tools, everything from axes to the first crawler tractors and indeed bulldozers ever seen in the North of Scotland. All sort of shortages arose and a new breed of entrepreneur appeared to meet the needs. The first thing the young loggers wanted was to be decently dressed for Saturday nights out. A small car laden with suits, despite the clothes rationing, made the rounds of the logging camps. Trade was brisk and not further to complicate transactions already suffering from language difficulties, (many Canadians were French-speaking only), our tailor friend pegged a $6 suit at Quebec prices to £6.

The next big purchase on our colonial's mind was a bicycle to get to the dance with his new suit on. That was a little more difficult, because bicycles were rationed at two per shop per month. However, there were no restrictions on bicycle parts and our happy bicycle agent was soon mass-producing cycles in his back shop to try to meet demand. Newfoundland at that time had few roads; the townships were linked up by sea and the longest narrow-gauge railway in all North America. The result was that the Newfoundlanders had to learn to ride their new bikes, and in so doing entertained the whole village. Our bicycle manufacturer 'faced with warranty claims on damaged bikes' got round the problem by lending out older, stronger bikes for his customers to practise on.

Other areas of free enterprise got out of control. A garage at the entrance of the village had been taken over by the military as their fuel depot. Early one morning, it went up in flames on the day of the monthly audit. That was a greater disaster to the local illicit petrol consumers than Dunkirk.

Based in the railway goods yard at Ballater Station was Milne the carrier. Col Milne had built up his Deeside business between the wars and had yards also in Banchory and Braemar. His operations had seen trucks overtake horses and steam road engines as the prime movers of his trade, although he retained both horse and traction engines until the late 1940s.

Col. Milne's traction engine

American International truck

Immediately before the outbreak of war, Col Milne bought two American International trucks, one of five-ton capacity and one of three-ton. They were the big and little Internationals of my childhood memories.

It proved a prudent investment. The colonel remembered and feared the requisitioning of private trucks as at the onset of World War I. He knew that, as the British Army did not hold spares for American vehicles, they would be unlikely to interfere with his fleet. He was proved right on all counts, and with the Canadians running International equipment all over Deeside, he had no problem with spares.

Chapter 5.

Tracks for the Times

It is the Age of Machinery:

Thomas Carlyle:
Critical and Miscellaneous Essays:

The Newfoundlanders' camp was built a few hundred yards up the Dalmochie Burn from the South Deeside road. I first saw it one Saturday morning from the cab of Col. Milne's big International, where I was jammed between driver and second man. It was on a coal delivery and we drove over the burn by a new wooden bridge that the Newfies had built, passed the old killing house, Ballater butcher's slaughterhouse, forded the Dalmochie burn at a higher level, then found our path blocked by the first Caterpillar tractor that I had ever seen. The roadside was covered by stacks of logs dragged from the hill above and, to my amazement, and clear memory, the crawler tractor proceeded to turn at right angles and then climb vertically over the log pile, clearing our road. As we drove past, I saw another tracked machine trundling down the hill, effortlessly dragging a bundle of long trees.

Caterpillar D2

The camp consisted of a long row of log cabins, each large enough to sleep 20 men. At an angle to the street was the cookhouse and beyond, on terraces cut on the hill side, was another row of similar log cabins, complete with moss-packed joints. Beneath the road were stables and the blacksmith's shop. The Newfoundlanders of memory seemed to be small men, dark and funny-dressed with long lacing boots and strange hats. There was a triangle set up on a tree with a strap to pull and announce lunchtime, but Saturday was half-day and everyone was coming off the hill as we unloaded our coal and left.

Newfoundlander lumberjack camp, near Ballater

Glenmuick House

The big International delivered only half her load of coal at Dalmochie Camp. The rest was for Glenmuick House, not the House of Glenmuick of today, which was Braichley House then, but the great Victorian mansion house of the Mackenzie family of Glenmuick. It stood at the top of an impressive avenue guarded by a lodge just beyond Bridge of Muick. As you drove up the drive, you passed a private chapel and scarily, a private vault surrounded by a railing-topped wall. We knew, I can't remember why, that the Mackenzie family coffins lay there, lead-sealed on benches. Round a corner, the squat, square house, the front entrance recessed in a bold portico and surmounted by a square tower, 75 feet in height, lay before us. Glenmuick House was typical of the great lodges that sprang up in the 1850s after Balmoral Castle was built, albeit Glenmuick House took on a Gothic style. That 1940s day, soldiers were very much in evidence. The house had been requisitioned by the military and the horses, trucks, hay, stores and mud would have driven the old-time gardeners to drink. There was an air of neglect all around: the great house looked sad, even doomed. I was forever sorry that I had to remember it that way. We tipped our sacks of coal down a round iron manhole on the ground and went home.

Chapter 6.

Chute to kill

Venit mors velociter [Death comes swiftly]
Rapit nos atrociter [Seizes us atrociously]:
                                    Student anthem

The Canadians had a much greater presence on Deeside. They built a large modern sawmill at Abergeldie and proceeded to cut all the accessible trees on Creag Ghiubhais and every single tree on Creag nam Ban.

Entrance to Canadian camp at Abergeldie

Beyond Braemar, they built a large camp and sawmill at Mar Lodge. Indeed, they threw a log bridge across the Dee, just above Inverey, to give their huge trucks a shorter trip to the station at Ballater. That bridge survived into the 1960s when the estate owners of the day had it demolished to discourage walkers from using it as a short cut to the mountains.

Canadian log bridge over River Dee

At Ballater Station, the Canadians built their own loading bank, where they loaded their logs direct into the railway wagons. They also built a log-cabin office to control shipments.

On the subject of engine power, the Canadians found Creag nam Ban above Abergeldie Castle too steep and rocky to log with their tractors. The solution was to place a petrol-driven winch right on the top of the hill, and, by an arrangement of cables, pull the trees up to a chute constructed of logs on the West side of the hill. The trees were duly delivered at high speed down that chute to the roadside, but not without loss of life. One morning there was a log jam on the chute. A Canadian Forestry Corps officer climbed up on the chute to clear the blockage: unknown to him, the next batch of logs was already on its way.

He was killed outright and thrown to the ground, where he was left covered by a greatcoat till lunch break. Such were the pressures of war-time production and the then low cost of human life.

The 70hp petrol engine that powered that winch was made by Chrysler. While it was hoisting logs on Deeside in the early 1940s, a sister and identical Chrysler engine was powering Ernest Hemingway's cabin cruiser, Pilar, out of the Florida Keys running on US Government petrol, supposedly on anti-submarine duties, but actually subsidising Hemingway's great passion for game fishing.

Chapter 7.

The Human Cost

What conscience dictates to be done
Or warns me not to do:

Alexander Pope: The Universal Prayer

From the start, there had been disquiet in the village as it became obvious that, compared with pre-war, wages had rocketed. That was attracting outsiders to fill jobs that local men serving in the armed forces normally would have enjoyed. Canadian and Newfoundland personnel were accepted, but conscientious objectors were despised and publicly accused of 'hiding behind the trees' as more and more were drafted into timber control work. The 'conchies' were careful to avoid pubs and other social gatherings.

Human tragedy took strange form. It had been identified that pilfering was going on within the railway goods yard, but the culprit, a railway worker, went undiscovered until one day he had broken into a goods wagon, found a consignment of whisky and was well intoxicated when he realised that the wagon had been coupled up and moving away. As he attempted to clamber down, he slipped, and his foot was crushed under a wheel. On discovery, he confessed to his part in all the other thefts that had put all railway staff under suspicion for some time. He lost his foot.

A sawmill worker got his calling-up papers and promptly 'slipped' and lost the first two fingers of his right hand to a circular saw. 'I canna sheet noo,' he said, and officialdom gave up.

Even more tragically, one conscript came home on embarkation leave and refused to return to his regiment. The 'Redcaps', military police, arrived and after his request to go upstairs to dress, a shot rang out and the village was quiet for a time.

Woolmanhill Hospital in Aberdeen was the medical examination centre for prospective conscripts. An unwilling examinee spent the time between coming off the Ballater train at Aberdeen Station and presenting himself to the examination board, in running up and down the flights of stairs from the

Green up to Union Street so many times that the board had little difficulty in pronouncing him medically unfit for military service.

One day, a barrage balloon trailing a broken cable came floating low over the Coyles of Muick. A woodcutter working on Craiglea foolishly grabbed the wire cable: it cut his hands to pieces. The Canadians at Abergeldie took great delight in shooting the errant balloon down.

There was great excitement another day when an aeroplane made a forced landing on the golf course and ended up beside the Roman Catholic chapel on Golf Road. It was a large twin-engined machine, standing on two huge wheels, with great propellers like windmills and quite hopelessly stranded. Next to the plane was a very large square army tent filled with bale upon bale of hay to feed the horses in the adjacent stables. RAF personnel arrived at that point to take charge of their wayward bomber and we were relegated to spending the rest of the evening playing in the hay tent hunting rats. By noon next day, our plane was transported away wingless.

There were many more tragic accidents with aircraft in the surrounding hills. One Whitley bomber overshot a forced landing in fields and crashed into Polhollick suspension bridge over the Dee.

The Canadian soldiers from Abergeldie Camp were drafted in with an International TD 9 dozer to help RAF personnel with the recovery. Lives were lost and the repaired upstream suspension cable mooring is still in evidence today. For many years afterwards, I was the proud possessor of part of the bomb-aiming sight, salvaged from the river.

We had been warned at home and at school never to pick up strange objects that might well be dangerous, but that advice was forgotten when we found spent ammunition cases from target practice ranges under Craigendarroch Hill.

Repair to Polhollick Bridge

Chapter 8.

Any any any old iron?

But Iron - Cold Iron - is master of them all:
Rudyard Kipling: Cold Iron

A great call went out for waste paper. That was responded to by all and Thursday was waste-paper day at school when the janitor was swamped with the week's collection.

The other great patriotic demand, albeit a much greater sacrifice, was for instant scrap iron in the form of ornamental Victorian railings and gates that graced the best architecture in the village.

An Aberdeen scrap merchant soon had men and lorries going round the village 'dinging doon' church railings, hall railings, garden railings, gates and hand railings all to add to the mountain of cast iron beside Aberdeen beach that was still there, unused, after the war.

The scrap merchant involved decided that Ballater was a safer place to stay than bomb-torn Aberdeen, so he rented a house and joined a baker and a money lender in commuting daily by train to Aberdeen for the remainder of the war.

Chapter 9.

Libation station

Drinking is the soldier's pleasure:
John Dryden: Alexander's Feast

When her brother was called up for service with the RAF, my grandmother stepped in to keep his job open. He had been barman in the Third Class bar at Ballater Station.

Station catering staff pre-WW II

The railway catering management said it would be impossible to have a woman at the rough end of the trade, but they would allow her to work in the First Class next door. She kept down that job for him till his demob four years later. On his marriage, he left to be a postman and Dolly carried on where she was for another five years. During the war she served soldiers, sailors, airmen, Canadians, Newfoundlanders, woodmen, railway men, builders, bakers, and businessmen, Poles, Finns, Italians, Germans, Jews and Indians and it was to her credit that she treated them all alike.

During the cold 1943 winter, she had mentioned one Saturday night that she was running out of firewood. Monday afternoon, we had three huge Canadian truckloads of slabs dumped in our garden. She would come home with wooden toys at Xmas; I still have a model barrow we now fill with flowers. She would come home with Indian chapattis baked over an open outside fire, but we never acquired a taste for those, as my aunts fed them to the hens. She would come home with American magazines, huge bars of chocolate and one day a Labrador puppy.

The Labrador pup

Although there was trouble at dances when soldiers came home to find Italian prisoners of war dancing with local girls, I can never remember ever hearing of trouble in the First Class bar.

In the 40s there were only two licensed premises in Ballater. The station with its First and Third Class bars, licensed to sell liquor till one hour after the last train of the day reached the terminus, usually closed at 9pm.

At the other end of the village, the old coaching inn, then the Invercauld Hotel, run by DC Logan (now the Monaltrie Flats), boasted a rather inaccessible cocktail bar within the hotel. Built on outside was a long saloon called the Tink Bar, a testimony to its customers, and the proximity to a strip of common land on the bank of the Dee where the itinerant fraternity

The Tink Bar regulars

regularly pitched their camps and grazed their ponies while in the locality. One entered the Tink Bar through a porch, turned right and was met by a frontier scene. The bar ran from a large fireplace, where long entrenched habitués had pride of place, the only seats, and where they heated their stout with the poker, fried kippers on the coal shovel and played endless games of dominoes. Moving along, the bar counter formed a three-sided alcove that was the domain of the hardest drinkers; the woodcutters, poachers, labourers, the part-time bookmaker and any incomer craving acceptance to the inner circle, which was granted till his funds ran out. Here poached game and fish and the spoils of petty crime found outlets, dogs and ferrets changed hands and illicit army fuel and equipment were sold. From this bastion the long bar stretched to the primitive toilet's door, the human pecking order descending through tradesmen, bus drivers, railway staff, youths, the military and finally the tinks, isolated, noisy and Irish.

Two miles out of Ballater the Pannanich Wells Hotel had come into being in the age of spas and the taking of curative waters.

The local laird, one Farquharson of Monaltrie House, developed the wells after an old woman suffering from disease had a vision of a white serpent drinking from a spring. She painfully made daily pilgrimages to drink that water on Pannanich Hill and was miraculously cured.

The Pannanich Wells Hotel

As the reputation for the waters spread, the popularity of the wells grew and the hotel was built with bath house and wells. Pressure of access and accommodation led to the bridging of the Dee and the developing of Ballater.

After heady hey-days and the well-documented visits of the young Lord Byron and later Queen Victoria, Pannanich went to sleep until legislation on bona fide travellers and the Second World War.

The sudden return to prosperity came with 24-hour Sunday opening and the unexpected bonus of the Newfoundlander logging camp. Mine host at Pannanich had taken the hotel on retiring from a career with South American railways, little thinking of the varied clientele for whom he would have to cater.

A Nissen hut sat behind the hotel wedged in beneath old beech trees of grander days. That hut was allegedly an office for Newfoundland officers billeted in the hotel, but I can remember it only as a function room for crowded dances. A deadly dance floor it was at weddings as the guests got lost and fell all over the place trying to stagger their way from bar to war-time blacked-out Nissen hut.

The tiny bar-room overflowed every Sunday, seats outside giving a panoramic view of the Dee Valley below.

I will digress: let us take a closer look at the panorama afforded by that stretch of the valley beneath Pannanich. To view from above always excites the senses and, subconsciously, one gains knowledge from the past, so here is a classroom for aestheticism.

We can see ancient Tullich Church with its oval churchyard wall giving away its pagan past; there the early Christian missionaries, rather than discourage the people that had been coming there 'since the ice went away' from deserting their traditional holy places, simply annexed them, and by hanging up an 'under new management' sign, introduced Christianity to Deeside.

The far sky-line is pure Morven; Byron's Morven of the snows. The foothills before us and rising from the valley floor are pure granite, cut and terraced by several quarries that have not been worked for so long that they no longer offend, yet still glory individually in names like Prince Charlie, no association with a certain bonny Prince, but the owner of the lease to quarry building stone there, one Charles Stewart, master mason.

Kirk o'Tullich

Ballater stone came out of those hills continuously from the 1840s till the Great War, then intermittently till last worked in 1946. The masons worked all winter in the Cambus quarries, blasting out great granite blocks, then cutting and dressing them into the lintels, sills and doorsteps you see in the Victorian and Edwardian villas of Braemar and Queens Road today. The method of cutting those rocks was making a row of holes by hand-held drill and heavy hammer, filling the holes with water, plugging the holes with wood,and letting the frosty air of a winter night freeze, expand the water, and neatly split the great stone. Whole houses were cut as numbered stones, to be carted to Ballater in the spring and soon built like giant play blocks.

Quarriers and Masons in Cambus Quarry

The Cambus quarries had a blacksmith's shop to sharpen tools, repair lifting equipment and chains, and keep the draught horses in shoes. There was a magazine to store explosives and mix the blasting powder. Health and Safety control was over one hundred years away, and the usual method of removing flying particles of stone, called fires, from a mason's eye was to screw back the eye lid by twisting it round a match-stick, then flicking out the fragment with the sharp point of a knife blade.

The railway also left its mark. Traction engines ran into the quarries to source stone for stations, bridges and crushed metal for ballast on the line.

Heavy Haulage

Across the road from the quarries was the bobbin mill. That industry was based on the ready supply of birch trees, the water power for the machinery and Great Britain's monopoly of commerce under the Indian Raj.

The Cambus-manufactured birch bobbins were used in the jute mills of Dundee and latterly India, forming a return cargo on ships that had brought in the jute. The huge boiler that provided the steam to kiln-dry the bobbins was safely transported North across the Tay Railway Bridge the day before it collapsed, on the night of Sunday December 28th 1879, taking a train with it.

All the above enterprise ended when Gandhi's followers led India to Independence after WWII, and terminated all outside contracts, but the writing was already on the wall for birch bobbins as the industry switched to plastic.

Beside the gates to the Cambus quarries is a steel drilling pipe with a padlocked cap protruding out of the ground. That is the hard evidence of a bore-hole drilled in the granite to establish if the rock could support a hot water injection system based on the inherent heat of the rock at depth. It had long been observed that snow melted faster off the Culblean granite than the older gabbros of Morven. Twenty years on, no more has been done. Perhaps the growing threat of global warning will bring officialdom back to this very real source of sustainable energy that does not knock eagles out of the sky with rotating blades.

Bobbin mill

Tullich beneath us had been a settlement for a long, long time. Long before the Christian missionary saints, long before the Roman legions' summer forays and long before the Picts.

From our viewpoint at Pannanich, we can see the ancient evidence, A fenced-off section of the field beneath us protects the entrance to the 'Pict's Cave', actually a souterrain, a place of security to Stone Age man from storms and foes.

People had chosen that favoured place, and, depending on the natural rhythm of the seasons, were hunter/gatherers. The wealth of plants, berries and fruit added to their diet of fish from the river and sustained them till winter and snow made weakened and hungry animals an easier prey. As usually happens in favoured locations, the population grew, and with growth came development. Stone Age had been succeeded by the more technological Bronze Age. Surrounded by a mineral province on the edge of the Lochnagar granite, early man on Deeside became a prospector to find and smelt the copper, zinc and tin essential to his culture. In time, the Iron Age superseded the Bronze and the pattern was set for the small farming communities that survive yet.

Tullich had its own market and was a thriving village until Ballater sprung up at the new bridge over the Dee. Later the advent of Balmoral and a railway that didn't stop at Tullich sounded an end to the community. You can still see the line of 'the puir hooses', where the poor, sick and old lived on the edge of the new turnpike road that drove through Tullich and 'dinged doon' the market cross into the road metal.

High in a birch-covered hill east of Tullich is a granite obelisk, built by Margaret to the memory of her husband, William, the last Farquharson Laird of Monaltrie. It is known by the old Tullich folk for their own reasons as 'the Devil's Darning Needle'.

The Islands of Tullich at the mouth of the Tullich Burn were historically where the Dee gave up victims of spates upstream and became a place to avoid. Ancient stepping stones led across the Dee beneath Pannanich. Stepping stones often feature in ley-line mythology, which leads me on to the slopes of the Crannoch Hill directly opposite Pannanich Hotel, where there is the Seall Cave 'the fairy cave' of Gaelic, in which it is '*Sitheil*'. It is said that anyone entering the Seal cave would come out at Kildrummy Castle.

Kildrummy Castle

Here we have evidence of a common Highland theme, the alleged link by underground passage of two noted points, often castles. Farther up the valley, above the mouth of the Muick, the Knocks Castle is reputedly connected by underground passage to Abergairn Castle built on the hill above the mouth of the Gairn, albeit the River Dee flows between them. On studying a straight line on the map between Tullich and Kildrummy on Donside, it is striking to see how many ancient sites of castles, churches and indeed standing stones are intersected along the way. That is the classic criterion of a ley line, one of the powerful straight pathways of the ancients. Ley lines, still hotly debated, would have predated any latter-day churches or castles, but they in turn would have been occupying older sites.

Abergairn Castle

Is it possible that there were ley lines to speed people across space and time? Tunnels were the only logical explanation at the time available to the superstitious natives? Should we be so sceptical, remembering that, but for an old woman's dream, there would not have been a Pannanich, and we would not be sitting here on a Sunday evening reviewing the past?

Meanwhile back at the Pannanich Hotel on our Sunday evening, the Morris 10 had been waiting outside and its builder owner, the tailor, the railway guard and the poacher got in. The car started up and set unsteadily off down Pannanich Brae towards Ballater. Half way home the merry Morris men decided to carry on through Ballater and on to Coilacriech Inn. We will catch up with them there.

Three miles West of Ballater, and several hundred feet higher, is that small coaching inn where in years gone by stagecoach horses were changed after the hard pull up the side of Craigendarroch from Ballater. Coilacriech may take its name from the hill immediately above, Creag na Crieche, hill of the shaking. That Gaelic name is most appropriate as two massive quartz veins intersect on the ridge, heralding a zone of faulting and instability which would be very prone to earth tremors. The alternative translation is equally tremulous: Coille a' Chrithich or Wood of the Aspen.

The little inn took the form of a house with a porch running the whole length of the front, supported by rough tree trunks complete with stubby knots where the branches had been cut off. It was otherwise a traditional slate and granite building, with windows either side of the door and a small skylight

Coilacriech

between the two bedroom windows upstairs. On entering the door, you were met with a tiny room: the right-hand wall had a wooden bench along its length, while the left had a short counter and a hatch through which refreshments were served. Eight people would have been a crowd. As in the Pannanich, customers spilled over to drink outside, but here at least they had a porch. On the other side of the road were the various farm buildings where the stables had once been, and as a concession to the 20th Century, a single, hand-operated petrol pump. Various vehicles were parked around, but many patrons arrived by latter-day stage coach, Strachan's bus.

'Coillies' had an unexpected windfall in the shape of a Canadian camp just across the Dee on the slopes of Creag Ghiubhais. Although the lumberjacks were working so near 'Coillies', it was several miles by road round Balmoral Bridge. To solve this problem a rope bridge was thrown across the river. It does not take a lot of imagination to envisage the acrobatics performed on the swinging structure a few feet above the swollen river on the way home.

Strachans Pre-war Albion

The Canadians were not the only casualties of over-indulgence at 'Coillies'. John Milne had a small Bedford lorry that shared with a black Clydesdale and four-wheeled cart the coal deliveries round Ballater. Time wore on and a new driver took over the Bedford from the one who had received it new in the 1930s. One fatal Saturday, a delivery was made to the Lochnagar Distillery, where the driver and his two mates fell in with a quantity of Johnnie Barleycorn. Next stop was Coilacriech Inn. The unholy mixture of clear still whisky of extreme proof and mine host's 'malt of the day' culminated in the faithful and never-abused Bedford failing to negotiate the bend at the bottom of the Darroch and ploughing into an oak tree, throwing out the driver and his two passengers to their severe injury, one worthy impaled by the hand on the garden railings of Darroch Learg's then garages.

Another episode of note was the demise of the Albion grocery van.

Drinking seemed to be an occupational hazard for van drivers, and stories go back to the earliest motor vehicles: their drivers' drinking habits were legendary and accepted. There is the story of a matriarch figure at Ballater station, meeting the car hirer of the time, and asking for a vehicle with a teetotal driver. 'I canna gie ye that, lady', said the hirer. 'But I can gie ye ane that ye canna ca fu'. Translation: 'I can't give you a teetotal driver, lady, but I can give you one that will not get drunk, irrespective of how much he drinks'.

Be that as it may, that van driver came home 'fu' for years. Indeed, as children we used to get great fun watching his attempts to garage the van behind the grocer's shop. That went on till the fatal evening he made his customary stop at 'Coillies', set out and managed to negotiate the bend at the bottom of the Darroch, managed to career through the village, but failed to steer round the corner at Knowles the Jewellers and drove straight into a telephone pole outside the then Temperance Hotel!

Coilacriech Inn was a dangerous place, but, to return up the hill, from its perch, 'Coillies' like the Pannanich, is a perfect place to have a digress. Facing south, the view of the Dee valley and surrounding hills is truly breath-taking. Creag Ghiubhais is directly opposite on the other side of the Dee. The old folk called it Craigendarroch's sister; note the feminine gender. Geologically, there are great similarities. Both rise singly from the flood plain, both are pure granite and both are classic examples of crag-and-tail moulding by glaciations giving both hills the same profile. The crags are downstream to the direction of the ice flow, while the long tapered tail upstream is the ramp of boulder clay the glacier built up as it climbed over the resistant granite, only to fall sharply over the crags to continue downstream to the next obstacle. It is that deep, fertile, tail of clay that is host to the scrub oak that gives Craigendarroch its name.

Upstream to Creag Ghiubhais is Craig nam Ban, 'hill of the women' a very different hill altogether. Craig nam Ban is not a granite hill; the rock here is much older. The granite on Deeside is associated with the Lochnagar complex and is evident today cutting through the older rocks, but Nam Ban stands alone, mainly deformed quartzite, surrounded by the granite.

Nam Ban rises immediately behind Abergeldie Castle. Legend tells of the master of the castle being abroad. An increasingly anxious Lady, being both concerned and suspicious, consulted Katie Rankine, her psychic maid, as to her husband's whereabouts. On being told that he was dallying with other women, the Lady ordered Katie to bring about his destruction. Katie Rankine went to the turret at the top of Abergeldie Castle and placed a bowl of water, with a wooden plate floating in it, on a table. Bidding the Lady to stay watching the plate, she took herself off down to the dungeons beneath the castle.

Upstairs, the Lady stood watching the plate floating in the bowl. Gradually she felt the tower house quiver then start to vibrate and shake wildly and more wildly. The water in the bowl was splashing about more and more violently and the plate was pitching around furiously, till, suddenly, the plate sank to the bottom of the bowl. At that instant, the dreadful shaking stopped. The Lady gave out a terrible cry: she had realised what she had instigated, and her Lord was drowned. The ship carrying him back to her had sunk.

Abergeldie Castle

Knocks Castle

Remorse soon turned to fury directed at Kate Rankine. She was burned in a barrel of tar on a little ledge, half way up Nam Ban, in full view of Abergeldie Castle. The little circle where Kate Rankine died has never grown over with vegetation to this day.

Between Nam Ban and Creag Ghiubhais is a peat moss; at a great depth beneath the peat is the contact between the quartzite and granite. These contacts are akin to the plate movements that trigger volcanic activity, but in a much more local scale. The vicinities of these contact zones were, although they were unaware of the geology, often sensed as evil energy sources by the old folk. Far from Deeside are the great lead mines of Strontian. The local people there utterly refused to work in the mines, saying that it was an evil place. That was in the 1730s. Time was to prove them right. As science advanced through the 19th Century, Strontian gave its name to a radio-active mineral found there.

The moss between Nam Ban and Creag Ghiubhais was also evil. Lights could allegedly be seen at night hovering over the peat, and it was the scene of Alexander Forbes of Girnoc's slaughter` of the seven sons of Gordon of Knocks Castle.

On the pretext that the Gordon men had strayed over the march onto his ground to cut peat, Forbes had the perfect opportunity to avenge a long-running feud with their father. He and a henchman stalked the Gordons, then, chillingly, set up seven stones with a smaller stone placed on top of each. They lay in the heather and waited; a gentle breeze blew down Glen Girnoc, and then one sudden gust blew down the seven small stones. Forbes had received his supernatural sanction; he understood his precept, no prisoners. The seven sons of the Knocks got no mercy, and Forbes and his man stuck the severed heads onto their peat spades. Soon a servant from Knocks Castle came with lunch to discover the awful scene. He flew back to the castle, where the news brought on old Gordon's death from seizure and falling down the castle's spiral stone stairs. Alexander Forbes's triumph was short-lived. In terrible wrath Gordon of Abergeldie hung him from his own rafters. His house was destroyed, and Abergeldie has owned Strath Girnoc to this day.

Knocks Castle stands on its knoll, with fairly complete walls but no roof or timbers. It obviously occupies an earlier site; people have lived there for a long, long time. As mentioned before, a tunnel reputedly links up with Abergairn Castle on the North side of the Dee. It is tantalising to place a ruler on the map and discover that a line from Knocks Castle through Abergairn Castle continues north to arrive neatly at the summit of Morven! The same line extended South intersects Birkhall House.

The stuff of Leylines.

Back at 'Coillies', the pub is filling up: the Merry Morris men have been joined by the newsagent and money-lender on their way home from a golf match at Braemar. With a few Canadians and the immediate locals, the scene is set for the rest of the evening. Around 10pm, time is called and half-an-hour later, the locals stagger home, the colonials set off singing the Marseillaise to cross their rope bridge , while the Morris sets off in hopeless pursuit of the newsagent's Wolseley.

Chapter 10.

Rail of the lonesome pine

Woodman, spare that tree!:

George Pope Morris (title and first line)

The Deeside Railway reached Ballater in Autumn 1866. The main objective was commercial, simply to access the great reserves of mature Caledonian Pine at Ballochbuie and beyond in Upper Deeside. The trees from these forests had been inaccessible since floating them down the Dee had been prohibited by an Act of Parliament after Telford's partially completed bridge at Potarch had been swept away in 1820 by a high river carrying logs. It has often been written that Queen Victoria stopped the Deeside railway at Ballater. This is true, but not through any Royal Command. Queen Victoria purchased the great Ballochbuie Forest for preservation and put it out of the reach of, and temptation to, timber merchants for all time. Why were the great trees in such great demand? Simply to cut into sleepers to satisfy the railway mania of the time.

The Deeside railway of the 1940s was the one we knew. Through my grandmother in the First Class bar, we had privileged access to all things LNER.

Since 1923, the old Great North of Scotland Railway had been merged in the group known as the London and North Eastern Railway. There had always been engine sheds at Ballater, but now long four-track carriage sheds were built, at the west end of which garages were added for Alexander's buses that had inherited the Ballater to Braemar road link that the old GNSR buses had pioneered.

When WWII came along the carriage sheds were put to special use.

On the 3rd.July 1938, an LNER A4 Pacific express engine called 'Mallard' set a world record speed for a steam train of 126mph down Stoke Bank. That record has never been beaten, and was the culmination of the rivalry between LNER and the west coast LMS that had seen ever faster times between London and Scotland all through the 1930s.

Dolly used to engineer treats; I can remember one afternoon we were taken into the carriage sheds. Four long bays of carriages were hidden there. That was the secret home of the Royal Train for the duration of the war. My grandmother led us up into and through the length of the coaches: today that is a memory of willow-pattern toilets and blue velvet couches and curtains. Next to the Royal Train was another set of varnished teak carriages. We were told that they had formed the train that had been pulled by 'Mallard' that record-breaking day.

In an age before the wide-spread use of phones, the engine drivers and guards just couldn't wait to get to Ballater to bring all the latest news and gossip from Aberdeen to their attentive audiences in the station bars.

My grandmother came home one night to tell us that the Palace Hotel, Aberdeen's premier railway hotel, had burnt to the ground, not the result of enemy action but a fire that had started accidentally.

The night of the evacuation from Dunkirk and imminent invasion, she hurried home to get my sister and me safely stowed under the stairs. Then she held open house all night for cold members of the Home Guard on watch for German paratroopers.

Evacuees from Clydebank arrived unannounced on the last train one night to be bedded down in the Victoria Hall until local homes could be found. The scheme, although admirable, did not take into account the emotional impact on the children or on their mothers and soon most were reunited with their families in Glasgow.

Another spring night at around 7pm, we heard a strange deep sound that seemed to roll up the Dee Valley. At 9pm, my grandmother came home to tell us that it was the German bombers attacking Aberdeen. Many people lost their lives that night of 21st April 1943, when Aberdeen suffered its worst air attack of the war.

Earlier Deeside engine

B12 Hiker

The engines that worked night and day on the Deeside line at that time were mainly of the standard 4-4-0 Pickersgill type built at the GNSR's loco works at Inverurie. However, my grandmother used to come home some nights and announce that a 'Hiker' had come in with the last train. I never did get to the bottom of the 'Hiker' till many years later. The 'Hiker' she talked about was the largest railway engine to run on the Deeside line, a former Great Eastern Railway Class B12. They were of 4-6-0 configuration and the 'Hiker' was a nickname the firemen gave them because of the distance between the firebox and the coal tender. Apparently it was so great that the firemen had to take a few steps backwards and forward with each shovel of coal while stoking the engine, so they claimed to have hiked all the way from Aberdeen.

Talking about engines, the railway did run past Ballater to the River Gairn. This short extension now makes a really delightful walk. The intention was to pick up trade from the Abergairn lead mines which were being developed at the time. A change in ownership of the estate and a very definite change in policy there stopped the mining and resulted in the lines being lifted and abandoned.

Much later, the first piped water supply for Ballater from the reservoir on the Gairn was laid in the line of the railway.

Our Family with water tank in background

That takes me back to my engine tale. In 1866, all Ballater took its water from wells. Wells in every garden had hand-pumped water from the water table. Then we had thirsty steam railway engines and no mains water. The railway engineers built a brick pump house and large water tank that was filled from a well by a steam pump. The boiler and firebox for that pump were sourced from an early locomotive, and built into the pump-house brick wall. That structure was always a source of wonder to us. The smokebox and chimney sticking out looked to us for the entire world as if an engine had driven through the brick wall, yet we could never work out why and where was the rest of the engine?

The impact of the LNER was to turn Ballater into a company town, and nobody noticed until everything stopped in 1966.

I can remember as a very young boy going to birthday parties at my friends' houses and being so surprised that there were no LNER plates on the table, no LNER spoons, no LNER blankets on their beds and no LNER towels. Very strange!

Chapter 11.

Dividend and conquer

Government and co-operation are in all things the laws of life:
John Ruskin: Unto this Last

In the late 1930s, the Scottish Co-operative Wholesale Society appeared in the more rural villages and towns in Scotland. The socialist concept of bulk buying and dividend-earning consumer membership had been conceived at the end of World War I at a time of emerging feminism and the right to vote for women. Ballater became a bastion of the SCWS movement.

The Co-op bought a large general merchant/grocery shop, an adjacent ladies' clothes shop, across the road a fresh fish shop (fish was never rationed during the war) and beyond the church bought a bakery and built a brand-new dairy. Co-op constitutional rules called for local democratic committees elected from the shareholders. With most men in the Forces, this meant that to make up the committee numbers the local housewives took over. Housewives, whose previous budgeting experience had been restricted to feeding and clothing their families every week on what remained of their husbands' wages by 2pm on Saturday when they staggered home from the Tink Bar, found themselves in positions of great power within the village. The town council activities may have been restricted by wartime regulation and edicts, but the SCWS committee of women ran the village undisputed.

The Austin 10 was pressed into service with the Co-op dairy for the daily collection of the milk cans from the local farms. In the dairy, the milk ran over coolers and then into bottles sealed duly with a cardboard lid. The bottles were then crated, reloaded on the Austin and delivered to shops and customers' doorsteps. Around 3pm, a steam hose sterilised the floor, walls and bottling plant, steam being piped from a vertical boiler housed in a little shed. That boiler was heated by coal fed into the firebox beneath. There was a hand pump to maintain the water level and on top were a steam-pressure gauge and a glass water-level indicator. The little boiler could have driven a steam yacht, and was a cosy retreat on a winter day where we heated our pies on the firebox.

Chapter 12.

The Turning Point 1942

*One does not fight with men against material: it is with material served
by men that one makes war.*

Henri Philippe Omer Petain:
The Price of Glory

By that time, the United States had joined the war after Pearl Harbor and the Lend/Lease scheme came into its own.

Equipment came pouring in and our Col Milne, contractor and haulier, became the proud operator of an International TD6 crawler tractor. Another tractor was allocated to an Aberdeen coach operator, a most unlikely candidate for a lumberjack, but such was the idiosyncrasy of wartime selection. The local Timber Control Unit received the heavier TD9 model, of timber extraction legend. They blotted their copy book the first week, when the machine refused to start. They dismantled and lost half of the components of a perfectly serviceable starter motor: the problem had been a battery dry of water. Starter-motor parts were not to be found and the TD9 had to be ignobly towed to start for the remainder of its service.

The winter of 1943 was severe: heavy falls of snow drifting in the strong winds blocked roads and railway alike. Troops were brought in to clear the railway line and a Girnoc farmer, notable for arriving at Home Guard practice mounted on his white horse with rifle slung over his back, brought his milk cans to town by horse-sledge, effortlessly slipping along where great army trucks were abandoned.

In Banchory, the Canadians camped at Blackhall, faced with a thirsty, blocked-in Saturday night, offered the services of their bulldozer to clear the roads. That gesture was gratefully accepted by hard-pressed roads officials. Not till the spring thaw was it realised that the machine had dozed away half the road kerbs in Banchory High Street along with the snow.

International TD9

Blackhall Canadian Camp at Banchory

The same storm created havoc with the timber operations and made a dangerous job more hazardous than ever with run-away tractors and overturned trucks. Canadians at their large camp on Mar Lodge were diverted to transporting in fodder to feed the vast herds of deer driven down to their very camp doors through hunger.

Poaching was endemic to the valley, but with most of the gamekeepers serving with Lord Lovat's elite commando, the Lovat Scouts, and the rest piping at officer lairds' mess tables, there were more pressing duties for Ballater's two and Braemar's solitary policeman to worry about. In extreme cases, dozers dammed the upper tributaries to collect the stranded, flapping salmon for a welcome change of diet. There was also the illegal purchase by locals of equally illegal firearms that came across from Canada. The fabled story of a nickel-plated Winchester still comes to mind and the resulting poaching tales have again gone into local legend.

The same 1943 storm added a strange myth to the already mysterious high ground of Ben A'an. A motorised infantry unit had been training in upper Glen Gairn that autumn, and whether on scheduled exercise or some foray in search of grouse for the mess table, a Bren-gun carrier got into trouble on the scree slopes of Ben A'an. Darkness was coming down and it was decided to abandon the recovery till the morning. The hapless military awakened next morning to the furious onset of the Glen Gairn winter. Before the opportunity to recover the carrier arose, the company was posted overseas. The machine, according to local legend, is still there, a Mary Celeste object. 'a certain shepherd knows where it is', and, an 'old-time stalker used to lunch in it', and 'there is still a Bren-gun in it', slipping in and out of the mists of mountain, time and memory, sharing the high ground with other ghosts of lost aircraft.

The Newfoundlanders clear-felled the Pannanich Hill and all the fir on Craig Coillich above the old drove road that entered the wood at Dalmochie and climbed gently to above Braichley House carrying on to link up with the Pollagach Moss road that crossed the watershed to Mount Keen.

The valley ran out of trees. In the space of five years, 500,000 tons had been harvested. It is a sobering statistic that, 50 years on, we now have a single sawmill at Burnroot, Aboyne, that has the automated yearly capacity equal of all the many, many sawmills operating on Deeside in the war years.

It has taken 50 years after concentrated, subsidised, planting by the Forestry Commission in the late 40s to replenish our woods. We must not let them be clear-felled again in a 50-year cycle.

There were signs of renewing confidence that there would be a return to the normality that we as children had never known. The Daily Express was scoured for the 'good news' progress in desert campaigns under Montgomery. That progress was charted on the kitchen wall with coloured pins on the battlefield maps issued periodically with the paper.

I digress again; as the supply of trees dried up, the Jews' sawmill was dismantled and sold as quickly as it had appeared. All that was left was an enormous mountain of slabs—the outer layer of waste timber cuttings that squared the potential board material. The Jews neatly evaded their environmental reinstatement responsibilities by selling that embarrassment to an itinerant firewood merchant. For years he and his entourage lived in wooden huts on the site, sifting through their decaying capital, trying to sell firewood into a glutted market. Every now and then, the firewood would catch fire. Sparks from the nearby railway engines, children and spontaneous combustion were blamed for the many fires that Ballater Fire Brigade attended there, until finally nothing was left.

Chapter 13.

Soldier from the war returning

Peace is come and wars are over:
Alfred Edward Houseman: Last Poems

When the war was over, the men started coming home: some we had seen regularly on leave from home postings, others were strangers who had been abroad or who had sat out the hostilities in PoW camps after Dunkirk or Singapore.

The roadmen returned and carried on steam-rolling where they had left off in 1939. Only they had a new roller. After the Battle of Britain had been won, allied planes controlled the skies over Southern England and there were no more aerodrome runways to repair. It was decided to ship the Deeside and Donside contingent of roadmen, turned Royal Engineers, to Egypt and Montgomery's growing army. The men and equipment embarked from Liverpool but were torpedoed in the Irish Sea; local men perished, and Maxie Bannerman's pride and joy, his Fowler steam road-roller, sank with the ship to the bottom of the sea. Undeterred, the men regrouped, were re-equipped and set sail again, only to be torpedoed while crossing the Bay of Biscay. At the third attempt, the depleted contingent reached Egypt.

The Territorials returned to take over from the Home Guard under a sergeant-major, who also ran the Army Cadets. The war had affected everyone differently. Some returned with the same Deeside Doric tongue: others had acquired English accents, often a strange mix of Cockney, Scouse or Brum, depending on which regiment they had ended up with. Not everyone was happy to be home. There were men that re-enlisted to carry on a career in the armed forces, and others emigrated to the Dominions and Colonies. Others, sadly, came home to die: the will that had kept them going seemed to give up once they were back. Some fathers came home after long absences to find young children beyond their ken. It was a difficult time for many; in war-time school hardly anyone had a father. Now there were children with fathers and children without fathers. That was a discrimination that would never go away.

Chapter 14.

The Roaring Game

Glory replay for, may it be our joy, To gain the Bonspiel by a single shot:
John Cairney (18th century)

When you crossed the Dee at Ballater Bridge, immediately before you was the granite pill box and two paths converging at a common entrance to the hill. Both paths climbed up to reach the old droving road above to form an inverted triangle. The left-hand path, although steep, had obviously been metalled and led to a red granite quarry as it reached the drove road. That quarry provided the stone for Ballater Bridge below.

Curling Ponds

Construction of Ballater Bridge

The right-hand path was initially very steep until it reached a metalled road passing a monument to members of the Mackenzie family of Glenmuick Estate. That monument, still there, takes the shape of a white granite cenotaph with a central paved area and semicircular wall incorporating stone seating. Moving on up, the path reaches the drove road about 400 yards west of the quarry. Just beneath that junction were the Glenmuick curling ponds. The ponds dated back to the 1880s at least. Three ponds had been dug, all at the same elevation, parallel to and immediately beneath the drove road. They had been engineered to face both north and Ballater and were fed by a deep and laboriously hand-dug ditch from wet ground several hundreds of yards above. In my time, the curling pond was the first of the three, well-kept, square and neat edges with a clubhouse built on the North bank. That was a wooden building with a steeply-pitched corrugated-iron roof to shed the snow. Inside was pine-lined, with a stone-built fireplace and exposed chimney head. Round the walls were wooden seats, with lockers underneath to keep the curling stones: there was a door facing the ice and windows with shutters on each side.

A porch ran the length of the front, the overhang supported by three square posts: each post sprouted neat spreading legs 18 inches from the top to share the weight of a roof often covered in snow. A wooden bench for spectators under each window completed the structure. At the East end away from the chimney, was a flat iron-roofed shed containing all the tools and man-drawn ploughs used to clear the ice of snow. At the end of the building was a tall flagpole. When the ice-master deemed the ice thick enough to bear the weight of the curlers, he would raise a flag on the pole. That was the signal for all the shop-keepers in Ballater to shut shop and make for the ice.

The second pond was always neglected and out of use in my memory, but the third was where all the children and some grown-ups skated. Skating was absolutely banned on the curling pond and to have cut up the sacred ice with sharp skate runners would have been a mortal sin. Skates were invariably second-hand and pre-war. They gave hard-up parents nightmares because the principal method of securing them to our best school boots was by a screw that drove a spiked metal claw into the front of the boot heel. The addition of a soon wet and loose strap round the toe did little to help the fixture. The continual tightening of that claw, done with the winder key for the sitting-room clock, served only to sever the heel from best boots. However, many, many, happy hours were spent on the ice. Our skating pond had an overgrown island in the middle that served as service station for skates when urgent repairs had to be done. Skating was popular with the girls, who somehow or another sported proper skating boots with built-on skates. When the snow came as well as frost, we had a choice of sport, skating or sledging. Sometimes we didn't because, if there was too much snow, we couldn't skate. We had our own Cresta Run from the curling ponds right down the hill, past the monument, round a steep corner we called 'the loop' and on down, ever-steeper, till we reached the bottom at the pill box guarding Ballater Bridge.

Sledges were like skates, very second-hand or home-made. The wooden frame and platform were simple enough to have made, but the runners needed professional attention and a visit to the blacksmith. The last blacksmith in Ballater had his smiddy on the site of the old gas works. It boasted the usual forge and anvil, cluttered bench and vice by the window, a large drilling machine and a separate stall for shoeing horses. Outside was an open rack packed with lengths of iron bar and angle iron and on the ground an adjustable jig for shaping steel tyres to fit on wooden cart wheels. The blacksmith measured our sledge, selected a length of half-round iron from his rack, cranked up his bellows, heated the iron to a dull red colour and shaped it over the anvil to fit our new sledge. Once both runners were fitting to his satisfaction, they were quenched in a water barrel and drilled and countersunk on the large drill. All that remained to do was to search in a warren of small wooden boxes for suitable screw nails and to attach the shiny new runners to our sledge. It had been hard work pulling the runnerless sledge to the smiddy but now it just glided home and I couldn't wait to try it out at the 'loop'.

That smiddy had had a busy war; just round the corner the soldiers had built stables on the golf course for their horses and mules. The military had their own farriers, but pressures of time or complications brought them to the smiddy for help. The village forge was many times more efficient than the portable army-issue model and could retain the heat required to shape horse shoes all day long if necessary.

Other new customers were the Newfoundland lumberjacks working across Ballater Bridge on Pannanich Hill. In addition to the many Highland ponies, the Newfoundlanders ran a Caterpillar D4 tractor to haul the trees off the slopes. The lumberjacks made sledges for that work, many small ones for the horses, but the larger model for the tractor needed steel runners and the smith supplied them regularly as they wore out.

The curling ponds and associated winter sports continued some ten or 12 years after the war. The great sandstone mansion of the Keiller family had become an hotel and in winter the tennis courts were flooded to provide instant curling ponds. To extend the hours of play, and cater for those who were unable to down tools through the day, the proprietor fitted floodlights, turning the sport from a daytime to an evening one that invariably ended up replayed in Dick McLean's cocktail bar. That was his intention, of course, from the start.

Craigendarroch Cocktail Bar

Still there were die-hards that preferred the traditional sport played in the fashion and locale that the Ballater Curling Club had enjoyed for 100 years. However, their numbers were infiltrated by hand-picked supporters of the Craigendarroch Hotel's management and a low-key meeting agreed to that party's generous offer for their clubhouse. The clubhouse was speedily demolished the next Saturday and a 1920 bottle of whisky found forgotten in a locker was consumed on the spot. From then on, all curling and associated drinking were courtesy of the Craigendarroch Hotel, at Craigendarroch, and the curling on Craig Coillich died out.

Chapter 15.

Our lodger's such a nice young man (title of song)

Few could compare with Charlie:

Jacobite song

Mr Charles Sinclair (left) and friend

In those days, with accommodation at a premium: every household had a lodger, and ours was a giant. Charlie was a general labourer. The outbreak of WWII had seen him second man on Col Milne's big International truck, and his war service saw him in the Royal Army Medical Corps with a short spell in Nairobi, from which he returned with a collection of moths and butterflies and a tropical helmet.

He then became in turn a carpenter, woodcutter, slater, and builder and between jobs a gardener. I have vivid memories of antics that now belong to a different age. With so much timber cutting going on, every time the Dee came down in spate, logs were stranded all along the river bank. Those logs proved irresistible to Charlie. Sunday mornings we would walk over the bridge and seek out the largest fir log; an auger was used to drill a one inch diameter hole into the heart of the stick. Next a pouch was produced containing black powder, possibly traded from some quarrier in the Tink Bar. That gunpowder was poured into the hole and a fuse pushed in and then sealed with river bank clay. The fuse was lit from his pipe and everybody took cover. The next bit I'd seen in the cowboy films in the picture house many times, but still my heart beat madly as the fuse spluttered and sparked its way into the log. Then there was a curious deep thump and the heavy log jumped into the air and descended, as Charlie said 'in kindlings'.

One of his summer's jobs was cleaning out the curling pond. Every winter, curling stones fell through the ice, sometimes because keen curlers were trying to extend their season beyond the limits of safe ice and sometimes the result of genuine accidents. By changing over handles to confuse the original owners, Charlie managed to sell them when the ice came back again. Strange finds were made in the pond from old petrol hurricane lamps of early flood-lit matches to bags of drowned kittens.

Charlie's stint as a joiner had ended abruptly one night when his employer's workshop went up in flames. He freelanced on for a while with odd jobs, the most ambitious being the demolition of the 'wid yard shed'. That shed was a wooden two-storied erection in the middle of Col Milne's yard, and the very refuge of the travelling show family at the start of the war.

At one gable, the shed supported a very tall iron pole that was connected by wires to all the houses in Duquid's Buildings. That early technology allowed the numerous tenants over the fence to tune their wet-battery wireless sets to football results, horse racing and on Saturday nights, 'the MacFlannels'. Charlie demolished their aerial and their reception along with the shed, an outrage that festered on in feuds and fights in the Tink Bar for years.

Charlie was next a slater but crossed his boss's wife by introducing the teetotal slater to the Pannanich Hotel's delights. It was quite a scene; the slater's tiny Austin arrived home three hours late. Mrs. Slater came out to find that neither slater nor labourer was fit to climb out. A lot of screaming took place, and Charlie decided next morning that he was redundant. A summer of poaching, gardening, and pony-trekking with groups of young folk followed.

Pony trecking in Summer

The builder owner of our Morris approached Charlie: and for the next few years he was to be found travelling to work erecting the monument to commemorate the Battle of Culblean, building entrance gates and shelters at Invercauld House, removing and re-erecting the fountain beside the English Kirk. It was a busy, happy time for the old Morris and its crew.

Re-erecting the Fountain beside the English Kirk. September 1955.

When he was in funds, Charlie was a regular at the Tink Bar. He would come home about 9.30pm to share in our late evening meal of white fish, courtesy of my grandmother's sister who worked in the SCWS fish shop, or salmon, courtesy of Charlie's poaching skills. If things had been going well, he would come home singing and do his best to continue the 'ceilidh' after supper, but if his latest ploy had misfired, he could come home in a vile temper.

One night he was in an unusually bad mood. At weekends, he had been picking bags of fir-seed cones in Invercauld woods to sell to nurserymen in Aberdeen. That night he had learnt that his cache had been discovered and returned to the forester at Invercauld. He couldn't settle on his supper, fought with everyone there, and slammed the back door on his way to his bothy outside, announcing that he was going to shoot himself.

We had heard that before, of course, but there *was* a gun in his bothy. Since he had been staying with us, my grandmother had given Charlie her late father's double-barreled, hammer shotgun for safe keeping, on the premise that it was probably safer outside. The gun was very old and now an heirloom. My great-grandfather had bought the gun from a Jock Kilgour on his departure for the Boer War. I had spent long evenings in Charlie's bothy cleaning this gun and learning basic gun-handling skills while listening to his stories of white-hare hunts and of clouds of grouse that darkened the sky. That night, the family listened silently and counted the minutes since the back door had slammed. Then a single shot rang out and the silence deepened. Nobody spoke: then, what seemed hours later, my grandmother ventured out with a torch and returned to report that Charlie was fast asleep on top of his bed. Next day was a Sunday and, by the slightest of chances, my friends and I were on Bridge Street looking in shop windows. When we came to the tailor's shop, we were startled to find his large plate window peppered with little pock marks, and, on the pavement below, there were the flattened pellets from a shotgun cartridge. I immediately realised what had happened. The shot we had heard the night before had been Charlie firing up in the air in defiance at the rest of his world. His lead shot had arced high over the three-storey Loirston Hotel, and over the Co-op grocery store to cross Bridge Street and splatter against the tailor's plate-glass window. This flight had encompassed the entire block from Dee Street to the main road.

Chapter 16.

The Silver Screen

Certainly but not necessarily in that order :

Jean-Luc Godard: when told movies should have a beginning, a middle and an end.

Every Tuesday, Thursday and Saturday, the local picture house held two showings of the latest films. Those were known grandly as the 'first hoose' and 'second hoose'. Saturday also boasted a matinee in the afternoon, where children were admitted for the old thrupenny piece. The films were mostly American, lots of cowboys, Roy Rogers, Gene Autry and Bill Boyd, who played Hopalong Cassidy. The show consisted of a short film followed by the news, a three-week-old, censored version of the war, then the main feature film. An entrepreneur, named Mr Kay, had built the picture houses

The Picture House

in Ballater and Banchory just before the war. Whether he had second sight or just plain luck will never be known, but in the war years those picture houses were packed with locals, soldiers, lumberjacks and lovers every opening for five years. The building was constructed in a cheap 'art deco' way, strictly functional from the outside, but inside it was the height of luxury. There were carpets, velvet curtains, and red velour seats, ranging in price from 1 shilling, through 1 shilling 11 pence to the back rows at 2 shillings and 3 pence. As the war rolled on, the entrepreneur also held shows at Aboyne and Braemar in the village halls.

Probably the largest crowds came to see '*Gone with the Wind*' the queue waiting for the box-office to open stretched from Queens Road to the Station Square. After the war, the picture house carried on, though less hectically, until television took over and it became, briefly, a factory for plastic spades. Since then it has been a store.

Chapter 17.

The Churches

The gude auld Kirk of Scotland, She's nae in ruins yet!:
George Murray: The Auld Kirk o' Scotland

Ballater boasted four churches. The oldest, sitting quite magnificently in the centre of the village surrounded by the kirk greens, is the amalgamated Glenmuick, Glen Gairn and Tullich charge of the Church of Scotland. Tullich we have visited. Glenmuick graveyard and ruined church lie at Bridge of Muick at the confluence of the Muick and Dee. Similarly, St. Mungo's, Glen Gairn's delightful church, lies roofless at the mouth of the Gairn. We have a Roman Catholic Chapel on Golf Road. That chapel built in 1905 is linked to the story of Roman Catholicism in upper Glen Gairn, an enclave that the Reformation passed by. The original chapel was at Clashinruich on an old road to Corgarff long predating the military road of the early 1720s. A staunchly Catholic family of McGregors lived nearby at Dalfad, and it was customary for some of their sons to join the priesthood. Fr Gregor McGregor, a Benedictine priest and a son of the Laird of Dalfad, built the chapel in Dalfad birchwood at the end of the 17th century. That building was never completed because of disruptions caused by the risings, but McGregors were buried there well into the 1800s. Fr Lachlan McIntosh was priest for 64 years to upper Glen Gairn and he is credited with rebuilding the Clashinruich chapel in 1785 and a second chapel at Corgarff in 1802.

Fr McIntosh saw great changes in Glen Gairn in his lifetime.He was born at Braemar in 1759, the same year as Rabbie Burns, a mere 13 years after Culloden and at a time when the last wolves still roamed the glen . As a child, he would have seen the Redcoats, garrisoned in Braemar and Corgarff castles, that maintained the military roads, suppressed the Jacobite past and accompanied excisemen on their searches for illicit whisky stills. After his ordination in 1782, he took up his charge at Glen Gairn, where he worked till his death in 1846. At that time, winters in the glen were hard and the springs late. The days of seasonal tasks like cutting and carting peats were announced from the pulpit and keeping Christian discipline with a people whose heritage claimed freebooters, cattle thieves, whisky smugglers and Jacobites could not have been easy.

Each autumn, young men and girls crossed the hills to Angus to help reap the earlier harvest there before returning home to their own. Once a month, the congregation would walk across the Glaschoille to attend Mass at Corgaff and meet up with the Catholics there.

Fr Lachlan's house was at Ardoch, in a 'ferm toun' of 14 fire-houses under the limestone quarries on the Mammie hill, quarries noted, by the Victorian geologist Dr. Heddle, as being a source of cinnamon-coloured garnets. At the turn of the 18th century that was a community of farmers, crofters, weavers, shoemakers, a general merchant, limestone quarriers, a miller and drovers all bonded with a common involvement in the illegal distilling and distribution of whisky.

The lairds did not discourage the whisky trade, quite the opposite; it served to keep rents high and created a high-profit no-risk scenario for them. That all changed with the authorities granting licences to approved distilleries, thus slowly killing the illegal trade.

The end of the illicit whisky distilling left the glen people no longer able to pay the high rents charged. That change in circumstances meant that, as the roofs fell in, the people left the glen. Fr Lachlan McIntosh had not lived long enough to see Queen Victoria build Balmoral, but he had seen the upsurge in *sport*. He had seen Corndavon and Morven built as shooting lodges to reach the then plentiful grouse and he had seen the gamekeepers come, and the restrictions placed on his flock's right to a bird or beast from the wood or hill and a definite 'no' to a fish from the Gairn.

By 1868, the chapel at Clashinruich had gone the way of all thatched buildings in the glen; the roof had collapsed. A new chapel and house were built at Candacraig at the foot of the Lary Burn, not to be confused with Billy Connolly's mansion in Strathdon. That new priest's home was much nearer Ballater, and, as the Catholic congregation had been greatly reduced with the depopulation in the valley, there was hope of making up numbers from the influx of visitors flocking to Ballater by train since 1866.

The chapel at Candacraig proved only to be stop-gap. By the turn of the 19th century there were only half a dozen native Catholics left, most of the worshippers coming with the Grants that had farmed at Abergairn for three generations, a devout Catholic family. A change in ownership and attitude of the Morven estate sped the removal of the chapel in 1905 to its present site in Golf Road, Ballater. By 1907, the Grants had left Abergairn and Scotland for Canada, this the family of John Grant, who wrote '*Legends of the Braes o'Mar*'.

Fr Lachlan McIntosh is buried in Glen Gairn Kirkyard.

The English Kirk: there was more on Farquharson of Monaltrie's mind than just the creation of accommodation for his Pannanich Well's patrons when, plan in hand, he strode across the 'heather muir' that was the future Ballater, followed by a horse plough marking out his grid of proposed streets. That was part of a grander scheme being played out across the North-East of Scotland at Dufftown, Tomintoul, Huntly and New Pitsligo among other places. It was a scheme to get the people that had been there 'since the ice went away' out of the glens. There is the Episcopal Church, predictably sited right at the gates of the old Monaltrie House drive on ground donated by the Farquharson lairds. The 'English kirk', as we knew it, was and still is the Lairds' Church. My mother played the organ there after the war. Canon Adams, the preacher at that time, was also Provost of Ballater Town Council. His sister used to officiate as his Lady Provost at all local functions. Canon Adams formed a small choir, which gave my mother extra choir practices and meant learning a whole new set of 'English kirk' hymn tunes. My mother also played piano in the local dance band that played to Saturday night dances till 12pm, then next morning sat down to the organ in the 'English kirk' at 9.30am. Sometimes in stormy weather the power would fail, and that meant that Ernie Rattray, who stoked the church heating furnace, would be faced with hand-pumping the organ's bellows. That was a terrible penance after Ernie had been out on the town on Saturday night.

Funeral of Newfoundland Lumberjack in 1941

The Free Kirk: finally we have the Free Church, now an hotel. The stereo-typed style and look-alikes can be seen throughout Scotland, a product of rationalisation and mass church construction. 'The Disruption' of 1843 left the Church of Scotland divided. That was in effect a tide of protest against the aristocracy settling ministers in parishes against the wish of the majority of the parishioners. As usual, the patrons had the law on their side but, at an extraor-dinary meeting of the General Assembly on 18th May 1843 the Evangelical members left the Church of Scotland on the grounds that the 'spiritual independence' of the Church had 'been invaded by the decisions' of the Courts of Law. The outcome was the formation of the Free Church of Scotland.

One of the first problems facing the new Church was one of accommodation. In Ballater, the Invercauld Estate, on whose land the village lay, flatly refused to recognise the Free Church. Assistance came from the then owner of Morven estate, the Marquis of Huntly. "Cross the March and help yourself," said the old Jacobite.

The March dyke is still there as you walk up the main road out of Ballater, and the first Free Church place of worship was a thatched sheep fold, built where Craigendarroch Hotel now has its chute and children's playground.

Site of First Ballater Free Church, now Craigendarroch Hotel play area

Years later, Invercauld had to move with the time and finally allow the Church ground to build on Braemar Road.

At the time, the Disruption split whole townships, let alone the Church. Shopkeepers and local tradesmen could not afford to be seen to quarrel with their patrons and invariably stayed with the Church of Scotland. The general working class, however, favoured the Free Church. It is significant to note Ballater's Little Masons were founded in the year after the turmoil, in 1844. Was it a long-term recruitment drive to ensure future membership for the greatly-weakened Church of Scotland?

Ballater Little Mason March

Falling Church membership after the Great War, which had raised many questions about God, brought the two factions back together in the Glenmuick church after nearly 100 years of separation.

The Big Kirk: my first kirk memories are of Sunday school in the vestry, sunlight streaming through the stained-glass windows casting kaleidoscopic patterns on tables and floor, hearing Bible stories of Easter, palm leaves and donkeys. We very seldom ventured into the main church except fleetingly for christenings, but I remember it as having very high ceilings and being bitingly cold. The manse in those days was the original Georgian house directly opposite the church doors, just across the 'lang kirk green'. The minister was held in great awe, and quite worshipped by the lady Sunday school teachers. He remains a frightening memory, crossing the way from his manse, already attired in long black gown, his dark eyebrows, rising at the ends, serving to give a demonical appearance. One hundred years on, Ballater's spiritual needs were being met in a fashion that denied that the Disruption had ever taken place.

Rev. Melville King

Chapter 18.

The Schools

Nae after days are like the days. When we were at the scule:
Thomas Latto

We had quite a walk from the bottom of the village to school, or so it seemed, on my first day. Setting off up Dee Street to Loirston corner on Victoria Road, from where we could see the clock on the church steeple, we crossed the road carefully; passed the Loirston lock-up garages, and then hurried past the Masonic Buildings.

There were three 'buildings' or tenements in Ballater. Duquid's Buildings were on Deebank Road, site of the felling of the communal radio aerial. Coutts's Buildings on Golf Road had children's gangs who were the arch-rivals of the Duquid Buildings mobsters. The Masonic Buildings immediately behind the church were of a similar three-storey construction with outside stone stairs, now long cleared away to form the car park.

The reason for scurrying past was that, on the top floor, behind her newspaper-covered garret window, lived a local worthy's English wife. During WWI they had met in London and he had enticed her north with tales of 'hundreds of beasts that went to the hill every day'. 'The beasts', she discovered too late, turned out to be bees. They had a daughter, a beautiful child by all accounts, but on the child's early death the mother turned into herself, refused to go out, and spent her days berating passers-bys, especially children, from her eyrie.

Now Golf Road had to be crossed, with its Richmonds' little corner shop, then up Sclackie Brae past Ian Sheach's house. Ian was a natural artist, much in demand illustrating bills for dances and concerts. A tantalising glimpse of the picture house and left turn past another joiner's shop came before climbing up School Lane. The back houses and garages of the great houses on Queens Road backed onto School Lane. When they were built, the large houses were let out all summer to whole families, while the owners retired to the back house. So School Lane was a cul-de-sac of little gates and garage doors linked by high stone walls.

Election voting always took place in the School. Best to get across their policies and catch the voters at the last minute, Tories and Liberals set up booths in adjoining garages. Those garages had originally been stables and had hay-lofts above them. The garage occupied by the Tory camp was the base of the local waste merchant. During one particular election, a very obviously Tory supporter taunted the Liberal camp as he passed with: 'When does the show start?' The ready reply from Liberals was: 'As soon as you are finished in the rag-and-bone store'.

Ballater Public School, almost at the head of the lane, was a granite-built single-storey building set between two high-walled playgrounds. Two large rooms with high, too high to see out, windows backed onto the lane. They were the woodwork and cooking classrooms. Each playground had its gate, and the school main entrance was twinned, to be accessed from either. Inside were the boys' and girls' cloakrooms and separate doors into the assembly hall. The school hall was a large square room; on the left was the heating furnace, isolated from the children by a metal railing and guarded by the janitor. Plaques on the pine walls listed former duxes in gold-leaf letters. The three primary classrooms doors were on the right; straight ahead were two more doors, maths and geography classrooms. Beyond the furnace was the science room and on our left was the passage to the headmaster's Latin classroom. Beyond that Miss Gilchrist taught French and Art classes from the same room for 40 years. The rope to pull the bell in its turret outside was also accessed here.

Altogether it was a neat, well-laid-out building, but, by the hectic war years, far too small, and three classes had to be accommodated in the public halls and ante-rooms. Later a prefabricated classroom was built in the girls' playground.

That first day, turning up School Lane was like entering a trap, a path of no escape from the school at the top of lane, but it soon became a place of little desks and friends and pastel-coloured counters.

An earlier school had been at Garranmhor at the end of Dee Street, close to an old ford used before there was a bridge over the Dee at Ballater and used again when the latest bridge had been swept away and its successor was being built. There was also a girls' school tucked under the main road as it climbs out of the Station Square.

Chapter 19.

The Village

A bridge too far:

Sir Frederick ('Boy') Browning:

Francis Farquharson had underestimated the potential growth of the village and he could never have foreseen the railway when he laid out his original grid lines. Roads, latter-day school, barracks, all Victorian developments extended into a West end area beyond the station.

Those developments were accentuated by the line of the over-optimistic Ballater to Braemar railway that brought about the construction of a railway bridge that never bridged a railway, from Station Square to Braemar Road. Clinging to the bridge on two levels is a primitive shack-like shop. The shop entrance is from the bridge road level, but the store room and rear door are underneath, linked by a steep, narrow stair. The shop's construction was mainly wood with a corrugated-iron roof. In the war-years it was run as a dairy, the store house full of round, local cheeses, produce of the old granite cheese presses still to be found then outside the former milk-house doors of outlying farms. Upstairs, the shop boasted a large counter and wall-to-wall shelving, well stocked with produce in spite of wartime restrictions. A door led to a tiny adjoining room that contained a desk at the window on which sat a large telephone; a fireplace and a bed settee completed the widowed proprietrix's living and entertaining quarters. It was significant that her cat was named Quartie after a favourite quarter-master sergeant, who could have had something to do with the maintenance of her stock levels.

At the Station Square end of the bridge was a photographer's studio. It was an attractive wooden building, with a steeply pitched roof, tiny darkroom in the attic and a porch running the length of the display window and door. That window drove us crazy just after the war when the proprietor, James Reid, an ex-Aberdeen press photographer, took his stock of Dinky Toys out of deep, war-time storage in time for Christmas. After a childhood of home-made wooden toys, that was unbelievable, even though they were pre-war models. Jimmy Reid was well known for his studies of the Royal Family and we children knew him as the school photographer of prize giving and sports. Sadly, his studio and priceless collection of old-fashioned glass negatives were lost in a fire that originated in the adjacent Station Garage and consumed both businesses.

The Station Garage had been a rambling, wooden-framed structure built on a triangle of land formed within the walls of the Railway Bridge, Jimmy Reid's studio and the railway line. That garage was fronted by a large doorway, petrol pumps and a glass-fronted showroom.

The Willox family had owned the garage within local memory and I remember Charlie Willox as an old man, very well dressed, courteous, who spoke with a lisp. His sister, Mary, equally old, was book-keeper. The Willoxes ran a fleet of taxis to serve travellers arriving by train. Since Edwardian times, whole families complete with their own staffs of maids, cooks and even chauffeurs came to Ballater all summer and rented large houses. The owners moved out to the 'back houses' for the duration. The visitors hired Charlie Willox's cars and toured extensively; it was a good pre-war business.

In my memory, the taxis were pre-war Austin 16- and 18-horse-power saloons, but in the early 1930s there had been legendary big Austin 20s. After the war, the Willoxes sold the business to an Englishman from the Lake District called Braithwaite.

I can remember seeing a model electric-powered racing Bugatti in the showroom. The Keiller family had just sold the Morven Estate, and as Alex Keiller was a noted buyer of Bugatti racing cars, the factory must have supplied him with that working model. Today a model Bugatti is priceless, and I have no idea where that one went.

Station Garage in wartime

Royal Train August 1928

The station was the hub of the village; after the war, it was returning to normality, never quite regaining its pre-war trade in the austere late 1940s and gradually losing out to road-haulage competition and the ever-increasing car ownership till Dr. Beeching did his simple arithmetical calculations in the 1960s.

In the immediate post-war period, the trains still carried the mail, the newspapers, and barrels of beer, live calves in sacks, dead salmon in wicker baskets, bikes, coal, timber and passengers. Passengers varied from commercial travellers to school children. Ballater holidays saw full carriages to Aberdeen and back, but Aberdeen holidays saw extra train loads of trippers swamping the village.

Every August saw the Sovereign of the land arrive in the Royal Train pulled by two engines and being met by the Royal Guard in Station Square to the cheers of the assembled school children.

We had a special use for the railway. Each year, when the travelling fair, our old friends the Wrights came, there was great demand for pennies to use in the slot machines. After our pennies ran out, we would lay a line of half-pennies on the railway line: the train came along and we were instantly 100% richer. Had to be careful not to use our new wealth on the roll-the-penny stand, where they would be easily spotted, use only in slot machines!

Opposite the station were the Clydesdale Bank buildings, incorporating a shop. The adjacent Victoria Hall formed a tight quadrangle built on four sides with the reading room and committee room complex, the Post Office surmounted by the Albert Hall and local magistrates' office.

We, as children, had only memories of the big hall i.e. Victoria Hall. That was where the Little Masons held their concert every Hogmanay after the March and we had to invite partners! The concert generally included a magician and a short film show: the operator sat in a small shed outside the front door beaming the film through a square hole in the wall. The Victoria Hall had served as a picture house until the enterprising Mr.Kay built his picture palace in Queens Road.

The reading room was never the preserve of us children, but copies of the national newspapers were delivered there daily, to be scanned by thirsty regulars waiting for opening time of the station bars. I can remember enjoying the London Illustrated News, full of black-and-white photos of post-war events and people. The library was next door and the home of the only copy of John Grant's ' *Legends of the Braes o' Mar*' that I then knew of.

Upstairs were two committee rooms, the smaller of which was pressed into use as a classroom during the war and later. That was Primary 4 classroom and a Miss Maitland was very much in command. Miss Maitland was one of three spinster teachers — the others being Miss Maxwell and Miss Gilchrist — who had been teaching at Ballater School since the Great War and concluded their careers there in the 1950s. Those women taught two and in some cases three generations from local families. Miss Maitland was a strict disciplinarian and not unknown to throw blackboard chalk or dusters at her 'abominable' pupils.

Ballater School Class in late 1920s

The Albert Hall, above the post office, also served as a double classroom, housing Primaries 5 and 6. For three years in Primaries 4, 5 and 6, we had to hurry to the main school in School Lane to attend assembly, say our prayers, listen to the headmaster's morning talk, and line up in pairs in the playground to be marched to the halls. At 11am, playtime, we lined up again at the halls to march back to the main school for our break. Break over; we were marched back to the 'halls'. Afternoon followed the same pattern, but without a mid-afternoon trip to the main school, except for physical training day.

At the West side of the Station Square, perched on the start of the railway bridge and surrounded by the only cast-iron railings to have survived the wartime scrap drive was a sport shop that was a magnet to us boys. John Smith, proprietor, stocked train-sets, Dinky toys, footballs, golf clubs and airguns, with pellets called 'cat slugs'. Because of the illustration on the box of an obviously aggrieved pussy, we thought it our duty to shoot at such animals.

Perhaps as a retribution for the shop-keeper's contribution to the persecution of pussies, on the day of the Great Gale of 31st January 1953, the hurricane-force East wind blew in the shop window and then a section of the actual wall of the shop was blown out on to the street. Weeks later, after the winter's snow went away, table tennis balls were to be found half across the village.

Before leaving the square, the history of the East wing of the Halls complex justifies closer scrutiny. The ground floor was custom-built as the local telegraph office, incorporating the post office. Inside was the counter, providing all the normal PO services; beyond that room was the switchboard, where generations of operators had intimate knowledge of the burgh until automation brought back autonomy and provided the Postmaster of the day with the opportunity of building a new post office in his back garden, and creating traffic chaos outside in perpetuity.

There was a door to the rear of the old post office that opened on to Monaltrie Road. Behind that door and up some steps was the domain of the telegram boy. He was provided with a strong bicycle and a belt that bore a leather pouch. In wartime Ballater, he became a dreaded messenger.

When Queen Victoria first took up residence at Balmoral, state papers and mail were taken by train to Perth and thence by horse carriage over the Cairnwell to Balmoral Castle. By 1866, and the extension of the railway to Ballater, those mails came by special train, and we hear of an early steam engine painted out in Stuart tartan.

After World War II, that service was taken over for some time by helicopters, the first seen in the valley, but they gave problems and often had to land in the Cricket Park for repairs and fuel, especially at times of high wind.

Ballater Post/Telegraph Office also had the distinction of being equipped with the first tele-equipment for transmitting photographic images by land line. That facility was greatly appreciated and used by the world's press reporting on the Royals for getting their photos to Fleet Street.

The Shops: opposite the bank and moving down Bridge Street from the square was a row of shops. First on the corner was the newsagent, owned by G.M.Rezin, a well-known golfer and connoisseur of fast cars. A narrow lane separated his premises from the rest of the shops and fixed to the wall was an enormous thermometer, courtesy of a cigarette company. In winter time, first stop on the way home for lunch from the 'classes in the hall' was a moment to consult that instrument to determine if we had enough frost to go skating at Brockie's pond after school.

Brockie's pond was a long-abandoned backwater of the Dee at the end of Golf Road. That pond had a great fascination for us in winter as a miniature skating rink, and by the Easter holidays its shallow waters were moving with frogs and toads. That was where we went with jam jars to collect the spawn that soon hatched into wriggling tadpoles. The tadpoles were presented to teacher for 'nature study' on our return to school. Now, looking back, I can understand how Sheila Middleton's posy of Lily of the Valley was accepted in better grace.

Next shop down was that of Harper the greengrocer, a greengrocer's to this day, but then supplied with fresh vegetables from its own market garden just over Ballater Bridge. That plot has long been given over to pony grazing, but still, each spring the little field is framed with ranks of daffodils, proud descendants of flowers that had been bought in Harper's shop long ago to celebrate Easter in church and home.

Third shop down was a hairdresser's, Glashan's, quiet most of the week, but bustling on Friday night and especially Saturday afternoons as this opening catered for workmen on their half-day. The little salon would be packed, and even with two barbers clipping away, you could be sitting there on a wooden bench for more than an hour awaiting your turn. It could be an amusing wait; Irvine Glashan, barber, knew all his customers well and would keep up a flow of gossip, banter, politics or sport, depending on who was in the chair.

Looking down on that forum from above the mirror was a panoramic painting of the local bowling club on their green, artfully crafted with all the members instantly recognisable by their weel-kent expressions caught in the various guises and actions of their sport. I understand that the painting has survived and is now hung in the Ballater Bowling Club.

Jock Harper's shop came next. Jock was related to the greengrocer: farther back, the family had operated a livery stable and carriage hire. Their corrugated iron base, latterly a garage and now a store, could still be seen at the corner of Dee Street and Viewfield Road until very lately.

Jock Harper had been deeply involved with horses before WWI and had held a Royal Warrant for horse-breaking, and subsequently served as a captain in the Scottish Horse regiment. Afterwards, he operated charabancs, early touring buses, but by the 1950s he was an old man, with a walrus moustache, hiring cycles from his curio-filled shop, spending a lot of time in the station refreshment rooms and sleeping in an old railway carriage at Garranmohr. His shop has disappeared now, built over by the extended restaurant next door.

Beyond the site of Jock Harper's shop you can see a change of building style. Up to here the individual single-level shops were built gable-end to the street. From here down and round the corner into Golf Road, the remaining shops have been built as a unit sharing a common roof structure. There is a reason for that: after a disastrous fire, those shops were rebuilt in 1924.

Jock Harper's garage

The Kettledrum was the restaurant of our youth, well-known for its home-made ice cream and a focal point through the war for Canadian truck drivers stopping off for a 'caffee' after emptying their logs at the station and before returning to their sawmill at Abergeldie. Their monster Dodge trucks waiting outside at the kerb, patiently, like as many well-trained dogs. Alan McHardy, the ice cream manufacturer, came originally from crofting stock high up on Morven; his brother Jock settled at Ettrick at the foot of Mount Keen and was a legend in his own right for different reasons. The Ballater McHardies stayed in a little house round the corner from the newsagent, and there Mrs McHardy had caused a car-type mirror to be attached to her front-room window to enable her to observe what was going on in the Station Square from the comfort of her armchair.

Next shop down was a dairy and more ice cream. That dairy was memorable for the display of a large model lifeboat in the window every year on Lifeboat Day to encourage donations. That RNLI exercise was the work of a Captain Frai, 'RN (retired)', who had settled in Ballater, far from his native Torquay, to run a fruit, flowers and vegetable business from nursery greenhouses that he had built in the walled tennis courts of Oakhall House at the bottom of the Darroch.

Coulter's Dairy 1920s. Dolly Cameron, manageress.

Foden No.1

Miss Mercer's wool and cotton thread store came next. I suppose it must have been the original mill shop. The Mercer family had owned the wool mill, beyond the smiddy, at Bridge of Gairn, and presumably sold their products direct in the village. Next was a chemist's shop: there the lady chemist specialised in blending her own ointments for strains, skin disorders and her anti-midge potions. You can still find her work promoted but under very different labels.

At the corner of Bridge Street and Golf Road a large shop, Richmond's, was a draper's. Issac Wright's emporium was the next shop, moving along Golf Road immediately before the bus station. On Sundays, he played the great pipe organ in the church and much of his spare time was taken up organising the ladies of his large choir.

Strachan's bus station was a modern art deco building, modern in the 1930s and modern today. Andy Strachan had started up his bus company in 1925 and built it up rapidly, sadly losing his life in a crash at Meigle five years later while driving football supporters' home from a game in Glasgow. On his death, his widow, Mrs Helen Strachan, carried on the business.

During the war, business boomed with so many troop movements and the great influx of Canadian and Newfoundland loggers desperate to taste the bright lights of Aberdeen each weekend. Strachan's garage also boasted the best machine shop in the Dee Valley, and with the general scarcity of spare parts was busy rebuilding and fabricating forestry, agricultural and transport equipment as well as keeping the bus fleet running. Strachan's owned a total of 46 buses between 1925 and 1965, when they sold out.

Moving along Golf Road, the Co-op bakery was next, still a bakery, but happily much improved and rebuilt from the happy home of cats and rats that I remember.

At the opposite side of Golf Road was Leith's bakery; altogether a more desirable enterprise. Since the principal's death, Mrs.Leith and daughter, Winnie, ran the front shop, while brother, Dod, organised the bakehouse. Another brother, Bill, is remembered for his taste in yellow waistcoats and leather gloves, and parts in the chorus in the local choral society. The Glenaden Hotel, then a guest-house, now leads us past the church to the Loirston Hotel.

Loirston Hotel

There George Lamond and his wife ran a discreet business. The hotel was open all through the war, a haunt of officers, businessmen and home-from-home to Kay, the very successful picture house man. After the war, the Americans started coming to Scotland. No jumbo jets in the late 1940s: everybody came over by liner and brought his or her car. All summer, exotic American Pontiacs, Oldsmobiles, Chevrolets, Studebakers and Fords parked outside the Loirston Hotel, where we eagerly examined the speedometer dials to ascertain the maximum indicated speed.

On Victoria Road, between the Loirston Hotel and the Temperance Hotel, was a private house where an Italian prisoner of war had lodged at the end of the war. As a sign of gratitude, the man had painted a floral pattern onto the lower window panes.

Of the thousands of Italians surrendered to Montgomery in the desert, many came to Scotland as prisoners of war. As the Newfoundland lumberjacks had cleared all the timber on Pannanich Hill, they moved off to Speyside and the Italians moved into their camp at Dalmochie. First thing they did there was plant flowers and shrubs around the log cabins. The Italians were all homesick; they missed the sun, they missed the colour and they missed their Mediterranean. Their artistic culture was manifest in every thing they did; they grew vegetables, they grew flowers and planted exotic conifers. Many houses in Ballater started to display beautifully painted windows. The Italians introduced the local girls to manners and bouquets of flowers. They taught my mother to play tangos and generally drove the local men crazy at dances, but in a drab war-time they were a breath of fresh air.

Johnnie Greig, the local manager for Williamsons of Aberdeen, ran a tiny butcher shop next to Knowles the Jewellers. The SCWS drapery department and then grocery shops brought us down to Smith's the saddlers, also purveyors of fishing tackle, guns, outdoor clothes and catapults. There used to be a cast of a monster salmon on display, 42lbs, by memory. There we bought Stewart tackle hooks that caught mainly eels, lead sinkers, golf balls and targets for airguns.

Across Albert Road was Davidson the Butchers, a long established, father and sons business.

Next came, and still is, the Bank of Scotland building. The next edifice was also a bank, the Aberdeen Savings Bank, with a lean-to hut serving as another barber's shop.

Crossing Deebank Road, we have the Alexandra Hotel, with memories of SCWS Christmas parties in its then wooden annexe.

Knowles the Jewellers

Butcher's Shop pre-WWI

Three private houses followed the old line of the road down and under the bridge, terminating with Invercauld Hotel home farm steading. We have touched on the Invercauld Hotel already, describing its Tink Bar, so let us return to the Station Square and make our way down the opposite, East, side of Bridge Street.

Between the Victoria Hall and the Clydesdale Bank on the corner was Gillan's shop, again a general merchant and grocer. Like the Bank of Scotland, the Clydesdale had two floors of a manager's house above the bank and shop, giving the whole building an imposing presence.

Even in my youth, the minister, the head master, the doctor and the bank manager along with one or two prominent business men formed the hierarchy of the village, sat on the burgh council, were elected to be Justices of the Peace and generally controlled their own community very well.

Proceeding down the street we next came to Joy Cormack's sweetie shop, rows of jars full of strippet balls, boiled sweets, liquorice sweets, barley sugar and on and on. Once selected, they were scooped out, weighed, and sold by the pound, half-pound, quarter-pound and ounces. A visit to the sweetie shop was compulsive shopping on the way to the picture house. To accommodate her 'picture' clients, Joy stayed open till after the second house showing started at 8.30pm. An added bonus was the arrival of Shand's bus with picture-goers from Tarland on Tuesday nights. Joy's shop had been started in the early 1900s by an Italian family, one of the many that immigrated to Scotland then. The son of the D'Agostinis had married Joy's sister, and when they moved to a larger shop in Banchory, Joy was left to run the Ballater one.

Next door, a very small unit was the new shoe-shop of our war-time bicycle constructor. From there, the whole corner of the block, fronting on both Bridge Street and Golf Road, had been built as another bank, but by our time it was a restaurant with letting rooms above. It is remembered for the excellent Lyons ice cream sold from a small side room.

The 'big kirk green' came next, complete with fountain, opposite the war memorial. Crossing Victoria Road brought us to the SCWS fish shop. Fresh Aberdeen Fish Market fish arrived daily on the Deeside railway to be collected, sorted, washed and displayed on the marble slab in the window. A twice-weekly motor van today from the Moray coast cannot start to compete with what was part of our staple diet.

Next door was a ladies' hairdresser, and next again was the premises of our merry tailor, patron of roadside hostelries. Next corner building on Albert

The D'Agostini Wedding

Road had been a bakery, but in my ken a private house. Across Albert Road stands another block of four shops, shops numbers 2 and 3 having two-storey houses above them. First shop was that of Hacket the chemist, who doubled as a feared dentist and in the 1950s still owned and ran a 1924 bull-nosed Morris tourer which was totally bereft of front brakes.

The second shop sold antiques, but the owner had been assistant organist in St. Giles' Cathedral, Edinburgh, and soon took over from Issac Wright playing in the local church. Mr Thornton also gave piano music lessons, and in time he aspired to school music teacher, where he met his second wife, his first having flown to the sanctuary of the priest and his housekeeper at the Roman Catholic chapel, as she realised what was happening. The redoubtable Mr Thornton finally crowned his musical career by taking over from the great Sammy Page the bench of the organ at Crathie Kirk.

Café Royal was first and foremost a restaurant, but to boost turnover it doubled as a fish-and-chip shop every Saturday night. As the first house of the picture goers came out about 8pm, a great rush of hungry people engulfed the Café Royal before the 9pm bus set off for Crathie and Braemar.

For my part, I can well remember my aunt taking my sister and me down to the Café Royal each Saturday night for a plate of chips, bread and butter, and a glass of lemonade, and then we hurried home to listen to 'the McFlannels' on the wireless. The real rush hour came after 9pm as the Tink Bar nearby cleared its customers.

The last shop in the row was run by Jossie Davidson, general merchant and grocer. Jossie, of my memory, was an old man then, still holding the reins. I can remember having to attend an interview for a messenger-boy job while still at school. That interview was conducted by Jossie in his bedroom and him in bed.

Chapter 20.

River Dee

What pleasure were to walk and see
Endlang a river clear.

Alexander Hume: Of the Day Estivall

Ballater dates from the late 18th century, but the River Dee has been here since the ice went away. The Dee was our playground, where we paddled, and later tried to swim in the few really hot days that we were granted each summer. Swimming generally gave way to rafting in large bus inner tubes that we managed to scrounge from Strachan's garage. When the rain came, and the river rose and turned a muddy brown, it was time to go fishing. A three-pronged Stewart tackle was the preferred hook and, baited with a juicy worm, was a surefire catcher of many eels but not so many trout.

We shared the riverbank with oyster catcher birds, dippers and whole colonies of sand martins that nested in holes in the sand banks. We knew the red shanks' nests and the hollow-tree home of goosanders. Scarce, but still around were kingfishers. We were mystified to find heaps of opened, fresh-water mussels, totally ignorant of the itinerant fraternity's search for fresh-water pearls. The Dee brought down all sorts of flotsam; left stranded after each spate subsided were dead red deer and sheep, logs and whole trees. Hundreds of turnips one year littered the golf course, and attached to a dead salmon we once found a tag, which consisted of a glass vial containing a note that gave us an address to let the Fishery people know where their fish had ended up. There was a reward of five shillings, which we argued about but never did get round to claiming. We knew every rock, stone and pool. We knew all the stories of spates and floods; we knew where the river had last burst its bank; we knew where Susie Birse's drowned body had been found and we were there when Col. Milne hired a rope excavator to cut a new diversion channel to save his undermined house from falling into the Minister's Pool below. We walked in the twin swathes that the machine's tracks had flattened in the summer grass as it crawled across the golf course. We marvelled as we watched the monster dig out the gravel and heap it high in a row; we were going to forget about school on Friday, the day that our monster was due to break through and divert the Dee. It was an exciting week. We were excited, but the salmon-fishing fraternity were going berserk, and at the eleventh hour the Dee Fishery Board of the day got an interdict to prevent Col. Milne from diverting their river.

The channel of the new Dee, as we now called it, was never filled in and only in exceptionally high water did the overflow run through the diversion, but to us it had been a real education not only in civil engineering but also as an insight to the politics of the valley. In winter when it became really frosty, the river's flow was reduced as all the burns froze up, and, as the frost intensified, ice floes appeared on the water to link up and freeze across on the stiller pools. During the war, the soldiers used to truck the snow from blocked roads to Ballater Bridge and then shovel the load into the river. One soldier accidentally threw himself over the bridge and the depth of ice and snow beneath was so great he escaped injury. Studying old plans and photographs of Ballater Golf Course, which has been in existence for only 100 years, you can see how the river has changed course several times even in that relatively short period of time. That power of nature, as demonstrated by the river, had over time carved the whole valley we see today from a series of ice melt lakes linked by waterfalls. But to us it was our Dee, always there in the background and as much part of our lives as the picture house, school or Christmas.

Chapter 21.

Substantial pageant unfaded

This insubstantial pageant faded:

William Shakespeare: The Tempest

Aberdeenshire Education Committee in the late 1940s was committed to the development of Youth Service in the county. Nine Youth Panels were created. The Deeside Youth Panel's contribution for 1949 was the Pageant of Royal Deeside held on Saturday, 6th August. That pageant, with the magnificent backdrop of Aboyne Castle, took the format of the youth of the valley playing out twenty scenes from the history of the valley.

Aboyne Castle

Nine schools took part, from Torphins to Braemar, and the history re-created was that of the first inhabitants:

1   'The Reindeer Folk,' presented by Tarland
2   'The Lake-Dwellers of Devana', again Tarland pupils
3   St. Machar converts the people of Cromar to Christianity, this by Aboyne.
4   'King Kenneth II hunts in the Braemar Forests', by Braemar.
5   'Malcolm Canmore receives Macbeth's head at Kincardine O'Neil', by Lumphanan.
6   'The Knights Templar visit their Kirk at Aboyne', by Aboyne.
7   'Alan Durward of Coull inspects the Hospital at Kincardine O'Neil', by Kincardine O'Neil.
8   'King Alexander III pays a visit to Aboyne Castle', by Aboyne.
9   'Edward I of England receives the homage of sundry local Barons', by Glentanar
10 'The Battle of Culblean, 30th November 1335', Composite.
11 'Witches frolic on Craiglash Hill', by Torphins.
12 'The Battle of Corrichie, 28th October 1562', by Torphins and Army Cadet Corps.
13 'The Black Colonel of Inverey sends out the fiery cross before Killiecrankie, 1689', by Ballater.
14 'The origin of the Reel o' Tullich', by Aboyne.
15 'The Stuart Standard is raised at Braemar, 6th September, 1715', by Braemar.
16 ' Rob Roy Macgregor visits his kinsmen on Deeside', by Tarland.
17 'The Story of Balnacraig 1746', by Finzean.
18 'The young Lord Byron visits Ballaterich and Pannanich Wells', by Ballater.
19 'Queen Victoria lays the Foundation Stone of Crathie Church, 11th September 1893', by Crathie.
20 'Royal Deeside, 100 years of popularity', by Deeside Area.

That event was rehearsed for weeks and I think I can speak for everyone who participated in saying we have remembered it for ever.

The Aboyne Castle of 1949 was quite different from the restored tower-house we see today. The set-piece for our pageant was the 19th. century front that Sir William Cunliffe Brooks had built on to the tower-house after 1888.

We were conversant with Aboyne Castle; this was where the Unionists held their annual fete, and legend had it that one room held an awful secret and was never to be unlocked. Be that as it may, Sir William's grand façade has been demolished in recent time, taking its secrets with it, but that sunny Saturday in 1949 we dressed up as Highlanders and rallied to the Black Colonel's fiery cross and on to the Battle of Killiecrankie.

The Monument Stone erected for the Battle of Culblean

Chapter 22.

Saturday morning work

Saturday's child works hard for its living:
            A.E. Bray: Traditions of Devonshire

My early Saturday-morning jobs were helping the aforementioned big Charlie. There were always gardens to attend and grass to cut through the summer. One garden that springs to mind was The Beeches along Golf Road and doubtless called something else now. At that time it was rented by a Mrs McIssac and her army-officer husband. Mrs McIssac was a tall, raven-haired, attractive woman, noteworthy of having a mother who had married Lord Aberdein, and best remembered as the owner of a fur coat that she shared with her cat, who claimed it as a cosy bed. Most of the time we worked there the Bradford van of Col. Eric McKenzie of Glenmuick was in the drive.

The McKenzie family had owned the Glenmuick Estate for almost one hundred years. Sir James McKenzie had bought it in 1863 on his return from India. As Little Masons we assembled in the Station Square every 31st.December, marched out over the bridge and up the 'approach', as we knew it, the drive to Braichley House. There, in the winter afternoon, we would be treated to scrambling for pennies on the frozen lawn, then brought into a large shed to be warmed up with mugs of hot tea and buns. In the shed, housed up for the winter, was the fishing boat from Loch Muick. It afforded six or seven well-sought seats for our afternoon tea.

Years later, that boat was to cross my path again. A small child had gone missing and, after frantic searching, it was concluded that the only possibility was that he had been swept away in the waters of the Dee swollen by a summer flash flood. I still don't know why I felt that I should search farther east than the Tullich Islands, where victims were so often found, but something drove me past Cambus O'May station. We came opposite an island; the old folk called it the Bell Island. Long ago, Saint Marnock built his first chapel there, and his bell can still be heard, we are told, on Holy Days. As we have seen at Tullich, the Early Church annexed the earlier pagan sites, and at Inchmarnock was a large rock in the river bed, accessible only at low water, that had a needle head or hole in it. That hole was large enough to allow young girls to pass through in a fertility ritual. At that ancient place we saw a blue bundle. The river was still rising, and the police decided that recovery would best be attempted from the south bank. It was getting dark before the team of policemen, estate workers and volunteers launched the Glenmuick boat. All the car drivers formed a semicircle on the river bank to light up the operation. The boat was secured to a tree and the current allowed to swing it across the black, heaving flood. I shall never forget the courage of the crew that answered the ghillie's call for river men. These were brave men. The convoy returned slowly to Ballater, and again the village was quiet.

The Glenmuick Estate had suffered badly from the war. The original Glenmuick House that we had supplied with coal had been deemed too badly damaged by the Army to restore. It was demolished, with the best granite stones being used to build the first of Ballater's post-war council houses in our old allotments opposite the Police Station in Deebank Road. The Pannanich woods that the Newfoundlanders had cut down were also on Glenmuick Estate and the hills were sold on to the Forestry Commission for replanting. The estate was sold to a new owner who renamed our Braichley House as House of Glenmuick. Mrs. McIssac and the last McKenzie laird of Glenmuick married and left for a new life in Mull. Years later Sir Eric was buried in the family vault on the 12th August 1972. There was no longer an organ in the little chapel, and I can remember my mother being asked to play at the service: could she please bring her own organ? That organ was no electronic marvel in the 1970s, but the original pedal-powered instrument that had graced the newly-built Roman Catholic Chapel on Golf Road in 1905, and was used there until the Grampian Power Company started generating electricity in the power station behind the railway in the 1920s. When the redundant pedal organ came up for sale, our family bought it for my mother. That organ can now be seen in the Heritage Museum on the site of the old Alford Mart. Another garden we worked in was Greystones. It had the added attraction of an engine-driven lawn mower. Greystones was the home of Prof. Findlay Shirras. He was a member of the post-war Labour Government's think tank and it was commonly known that he drew up most of the principles of the National Health Service right here in Ballater. What would he think of the Thatcher-era rash of nursing homes that now constitute an industry in the village?

Prof Shirras was the proud owner of a beautiful maroon Lagonda tourer. It was immaculate. Equally proud of it was Alan Robertson, owner of the Riverside Garage, who was entrusted with its care. After the professor died, I can remember Alan Robertson saying: 'Well, that's the end of her' as the professor's son took possession of the Lagonda and disappeared rapidly South-bound.

He crashed violently in the Borders and wrote the car off later that day.

Chapter 23.

Playgrounds

O! many a shaft, at random sent, Finds mark the archer little meant!:
Sir Walter Scott: The Lord of the Isles

In the corner of the Wid Yard were a plumber's shop, office, workshop and store. At the end of that low building was an outside dry toilet without a door. We discovered an old bucket there filled with discarded lead seals from wine and spirit bottles sourced from the two licensed premises in the village. A good third of Milne's Wid Yard was given over to nettles all summer, a crop that was probably well manured by the burial of horses there in their days. The result was that in autumn the nettles lost their stinging leaves and became hard bare stalks. Those stalks became our arrows to complement the bows that we made from the annual pruning of the kirk green trees. At some point on our development of that weaponry, we discovered that wrapping a strip of lead foil, from the plumber's bucket around the tip of our nettle-stalk arrow — totally ignoring the fact that the plumber had full intentions of melting down the bottle caps for soldering lead to repair the oncoming winter's frost damage —made the arrow shoot much farther more accurately. We learnt a lot about ballistics in the 'Wid Yard'.

It was wartime and the news we saw at the picture house was war, war, war, albeit three-weeks old and heavily censured. Yet our exposure to planes, tanks and ships on film and Bren-gun carriers on the streets of Ballater and field guns lined up on the golf course made us six-year-old veterans. The older boys shared our Wid Yard playground and by sheer strength of numbers lifted the boxes of old two-wheeled horse-drawn carts and inverted them on top of the flat platforms of four-wheeled carts. That created a battleship with a look-alike turret. By cutting out boards from the floor of the lower cart and blocking in the skirt round the wheels, we could enter our vessel at ground level, pull the door shut and climb up through the floor into the upturned cart above. We soon had a hole cut in the upper cart floor and so had access to the 'deck'.

Soon we had two of those vessels commissioned and stocked with heavy chunks of scrap iron for depth-charges and large quantities of empty army ration tins for shells. The next logical development was war. Night after night, rival gangs attracted by our ships came to the Wid Yard to pound each other with bean cans and worse. I can still feel the scar on top of my head where a rusty tin drew a lot of blood nearly sixty years ago.

The White Widdie: Monaltrie House sat under the east crags of Craigendarroch Hill where the Farquharson laird had built it, squat, low and hewn from the rough red granite of the Pass of Ballater. That same laird had been instrumental in mining lead ore from the crags of Sgor Buidhe, the argentiferous galena producing enough silver for him to have a set of buttons made for his Highland dress tunic.

The house had long ceased to be a family seat as deaths, annexations and costs forced consolidation of the Farquharson elite at Invercauld House. Up to the outbreak of World War II, the Clydeside shipbuilding family of Yarrows had rented the house, then it had been requisitioned to billet army personnel.

Monaltrie House came into our lives after the war and after the soldiers had left it a broken, stripped-out shell. It was our White House in the White Widdie. We would never venture there alone, and certainly not at night. Only in gangs did we find enough courage or bravado to climb through broken windows to explore the dark interior.

The mansion house was built as two parallel buildings. The south-facing main house, quite long but only of ground and first-floor height, hid a similar structure behind that was built even farther into the hill and housed staff quarters, sheds, stables and coach houses.

Nothing had escaped the attention of the military, and why their discipline allowed the wanton destruction I have never discovered. That situation was not unique; Glenmuick House was an altogether much larger house, but the damage there was so extreme that the only solution was demolition.

We scrambled along corridors of rotting flooring, cautious not to fall through to the cellars, looking into rooms with walls covered with the first graffiti we had ever seen, and fortunately couldn't decipher. The grand rooms retained their sense of space and light, but here the oak panelling had been torn from the walls to feed the fire.

In one room, a large mural occupied most of a wall; the scene depicted was obviously done to caricature the Indian Mountain Artillery in particular and the Army in general. That painting showed an obviously reluctant mule being pushed up a mountain by its handler, who was in turn being pushed by a corporal, who was in turn being pushed by a sergeant, who was being pushed by a second lieutenant, then a full lieutenant, then a captain, then a major and so on till finally at the foot of the mountain, resplendid with top hat and cigar, Winston Churchill was pushing his generals.

Outside, the windows were broken, doors missing and gutters gone. The secondary wing had been used as a rubbish tip for the five years and whole sections were collapsing under the neglect, build-up of water, and the relentless weight of Craigendarroch Hill behind.

Upstairs in the south wing, the ceilings had been torn down to allow access to the swarms of bees that had sought sanctuary under the eaves. That access was not to retrieve the bees, but to harvest the honey stored there. In the old gardens everything was overgrown but proved a magnet for us where we could search for birds' nests and hunt rabbits.

All round the house were signs of the military occupation; empty ration tins by the hundred, old fuel cans, ammunition boxes and, in the pits dug for Sten gun practice, literally buckets of spent 9mm cartridge cases.

Not surprisingly, we engaged in war games most of the time, gangs from the bottom of the village near the river versus those that lived at the top by the station. The sawmills kept us supplied with wooden spears and swords while the older boys started to acquire air pistols and rifles.

An alarming escalation of the use of Monaltrie House came with the formation of an Army Cadet Force unit. The instructors recognised the derelict building as a perfect training ground for would-be commandos, and every Friday night battles were fought on the grounds with real .303 rifles firing blanks.

The White Widdie behind the station had been home to Indian soldiers during the war. To billet in the grandeur of Monaltrie House was not for them, but a camp of tents close to their stables of mules was their Highland home. Those tall, black-bearded, turbaned men trained with their mule-drawn-artillery in the Deeside hills until recalled to India and the Burma Campaign. The Indians did all of their cooking outside on open fires. Everybody shut up hens at night and worried about straying cats and dogs, but we can remember them baking only chapattis. Some of the boys became fascinated with the Indians, made friends with them, and were invited into their camp. Not all parents agreed with that, as cultural differences could blur the limits of accepted behaviour. In years to come, some individuals' deviations would be directly linked to the time they spent with the Indians by the philosophers of the Tink Bar. But by our time all that remained of the Indians' sojourn were the latrine holes dug in the gravel. They were definitely out of bounds.

The White Widdie was then a young self-seeded fir wood home to steam-powered sawmills, old wooden-wheeled caravans that were the homes of woodcutters, and a strong granite-built magazine that used to hold the quarriers' dynamite and latterly army ammunition.

Craigendarroch Hill towered above us, a living graph of how rising altitude affects tree species. In those days, the lower slopes were home to shrub oak exclusively, and as we climbed up the hill, past the early quarries, the oaks gave way to native pine at around 900 feet above sea level while the primeval summit was covered in birch colonising the ground after a fire.

Today things are different. Age, acid rain, Chernobyl fallout or climate changes are causing the oaks to die. As the oaks highest up the hillside, and already at their limits of altitude and existence, decay and fall, a new belt of birch forms between the receding oaks and the pine.

Now our White Widdie playground has a Primary School where once there were turbaned Sikhs, and housing developments cover the Sten gun butts.

Chapter 24.

Losing the plot

Let us see these handsome houses:
Alfred, Lord Tennyson:
The Lord Of Burleigh

After the war, a new Labour government was elected, much to Winston Churchill's surprise. The New Thinking touched on many aspects of social life across the UK and Ballater was no exception. Open ground known as 'the Plotties' opposite the Police Station was selected for council housing.

The Plotties were allotments where the locals grew the vegetables that had been a very welcome supplement to the wartime rations. Our family had rented one of these Plotties for many years and there was wide-spread opposition to the proposal to build on the land. First council employees, then councillors, tried to calm things down but it took a court order to remove the reluctant tenants, and only then after that season's bounty had been carefully harvested and the building programme delayed into winter.

There must have been a dozen individual allotments in the area bounded on two sides by Deebank Road and Dee Street, and, across the wall, on one side by a further cluster of plotties, and on the Western extremity by the last smiddy in Ballater.

Our plottie was rectangular, edged with boxwood, and growing in three of the four corners were apple trees that taught us how to climb, and by autumn gave us apples worth climbing for. Beneath were grown turnips, carrots, cabbages, cauliflowers and brussels sprouts, but the main crop was potatoes, early and late.

The Plotties had been there for a long time; indeed the Glen people moved 'doon to Ballater' only on the promise of available ground for vegetables denied them in 'the tenement buildings'. Year by year from the early 1800s horse dung was collected from the streets to manure the ground; the fertility was obvious from the gardeners' results and the depth of mould was revealed each autumn when we dug the tattie pit. That pit was dug on the side of the plottie nearest the gate; next we brought in loads of ferns in our cartie from the hill over the bridge, which were used to insulate the store of potatoes and protect them from the winter's frosts.

But it was the last year of the plotties so we had to fill our potatoes into sacks and carry them home. When the builders came, we stayed away, unwilling to see the apple trees felled.

Soon the activity brought us back to watch the first houses actually being built that we had ever seen. Those houses on Deebank Road were the last totally traditional granite-and-slate houses ever built in Ballater. We did not know it then, but we were watching the end of a tradition of local house building by local tradesmen and materials as surely as we later witnessed the demise of The Deeside Railway Line.

The uplifted railway line

The contractors charged with building the Deebank Road council houses were also busy with the demolition of Glenmuick House. That huge mansion had housed army units throughout the war and the neglect that I remembered from 1943 had only got worse. At the end of the war, there was a change of ownership at the Glenmuick Estate, and the decision was made that the neo-Gothic pile was redundant, even if it had been economic to rebuild. Glenmuick House, which we remembered on its north-facing site looking over to Ballater, was, like many other great houses in Scotland at that time, dismantled to salvage all reusable granite stone, slate, lead, timber, fireplaces, windows and doors.

The demolition of Glenmuick House

Much of the re-dressed stone went to build the council houses in Deebank Road. When that source ran out, the contractors reopened the Cambus o'May quarries for the very last time to finish the job.

The work of house building in the 1940s was very labour-intensive. Little men dug all foundations, drains and sewers with pick and shovel. Masons set stones with lime mortar and burnt both hands and eyes. Joiners sawed and nailed wood till they left for more money at the burgeoning hydro-electric dams programme.

Listening to our elders after a Saturday dinner-time session in the Tink we got the impression then that the building trade was not a happy one. The labourers always expected more wages than they received; the jobs never turned out as promised; the weather, especially at Ballater's 660 ft. altitude, often meant lay-offs at times of deep snow or frost.

The housing programme continued and houses were built on Golf Road beyond the chapel, and then behind the station in our White Widdie. We grew accustomed to the builders and their work but for us it could never compete with the timber industry. The fascination and glamour of the big trucks, snarling crawler tractors, the steep forests and the individuals that worked there meant that the building site would always come a poor second in our young ambitions.

Chapter 25.

The Air Training Corps

Per Ardua ad Astra [Through Difficulties to the Stars]:
Royal Air Force motto

As the war slipped away, the village tried to get back to its pre-war normality. Returning servicemen took up their old jobs, where they could. Many left for the dominions of Canada, Australia and New Zealand. A few could not settle and returned to a career in the Forces, and others came home to die. Most, although demobbed, could never let go and the Burma campaign, the Battle of El Alamein and the Normandy beaches would be fought in the Tink on Saturday nights for the next three decades.

Others had a different way of handling their civilian lives. Unable to re-enlist for one reason or another, certain ex-servicemen, mainly former officers and NCOs, finding the tedium of a tradesman's life an unbearable substitute for the glamour and excitement of their former status, reinvented themselves as COs and instructors in local flights and troops of Air Training Corps and Army Cadet Forces.

Those organisations found a ready supply of young recruits. Existing youth organisations in the village were restricted to the Cub and Scout movements and they were no competition to the Junior Forces. Because they were, in effect, recruitment schemes for the adult forces, the Junior Forces did not in the late forties suffer from lack of funding and the erstwhile instructors could enjoy regular forces pay while at annual camp and on courses, and indeed could count on generous bounties for any cadet that went on to join the boy entry scheme.

The ATC tended to attract the brightest boys, primarily targeted as, and later trained as, potential aircrew, pilots, navigators and wireless operators. Dyce aerodrome was still an RAF base and Aberdeen Airport was still twenty years away. Dyce RAF Station of the late forties/early fifties was still flying Avro Anson transports and the University Air Squadron were learning to fly in DeHavilland Chipmunk trainers. It was rumoured that a Mitchell bomber still lurked in one of the hangars.

Sunday morning saw us travel by bus to Aberdeen — no trains on Sundays — get off at the Wallace Statue and catch another bus to Dyce. We wore our blue ATC uniforms with our knives, forks and spoons tucked into the special deep pocket inside our tunics. Dyce air base was cold, windy, and wet. The buildings were war-time corrugated iron huts and two huge hangars. One Avro Anson stood on the concrete, its flaps fluttering in the wind. A flight of Chipmunks was lined up looking tiny and fragile, while a Tiger Moth bi-plane with open cockpit and a spider's web of wires holding everything together looked decidedly dated and unsafe. We were glad that our visit was restricted to an inter-squadron Aircraft Recognition Contest.

Ballater ATC squadron 2240 won the northern section Aircraft Recognition Contest and that meant that we now would have to compete in the Finals at RAF Turnhouse, Edinburgh, later that month. But first it was off to the mess hall for a late lunch.

The Turnhouse trip meant that our little team of four cadets accompanied by two officers travelled down to Edinburgh by train from Aberdeen on a Saturday. The contest was held on the Sunday morning and we were to return Sunday afternoon. The train journey south was memorable for my first sight and crossing of the Forth Railway Bridge. Our officers travelled first-class while we were issued with third-class tickets, and when we arrived at Princes Street station an RAF truck took us to Turnhouse. We never saw our officers again till we arrived back in Aberdeen on Sunday night. Apparently they had spent some time in Edinburgh before staying at the officers' mess at Turnhouse overnight and returning first-class to Aberdeen.

One of my team-mates had an uncle and aunt in Edinburgh: they collected us from camp in their then new Jaguar car and we spent a pleasant Saturday night at their home. As they drove us back to camp, the guard at Turnhouse gate sprang to attention and saluted a shiny Jaguar containing two very small cadets.

The absent officers who should have been in charge of the team forgot to let the mess officer know that we were on the camp, with the result we were not on the ration list and could not get any food in the canteen. We existed for the rest of the weekend on Kit-Kats and Cola bought with our own money from the NAAFI. Next day we lost the competition to a Glasgow team and returned home over the Forth Bridge.

A.T.C. Certificate

Chapter 26.

Secondary School

Whilst the Latin, queen of tongues, Is not yet free from rhyme's wrongs, But rests foiled:
Ben Jonson: A Fit of Rhyme against Rhyme

Secondary school at Ballater was back where we started at the top of School Lane. In the years between 1943 and now 1953, World War II had been fought and won. There was still food rationing and indeed the senior pupils had the job of distributing the ration books and filling out the names and addresses on the new books. Our headmaster had started at Ballater School the same year as we did in 1943, taking over from Mr Chisholm, who had taught my mother. Mr J.P.Craig, his successor, grew his own pipe tobacco, loved to fish and was a classics scholar. His second-in-command was the Miss Gilchrist who taught French and Art from the same classroom for 40 years. Into their tender mercies was placed our secondary education. J.P.Craig's idea of education was the path to the classics. On that premise, we were fed Latin at a time it was being dropped at almost every other school in the county.

The year 1953 was quite memorable; on the 31st January an East wind blew down great numbers of trees all over the North-East of Scotland, and after the death of King George VI, we had a Coronation to celebrate on 2nd June.

We spent hours on top of Craigendarroch gathering firewood from the mass of blown-down trees on the hill to form a giant Coronation Bonfire that seemingly would burn forever. The 700-foot climb each night never bothered us at that age, and I can remember four minutes being recorded as the time it took us one Friday night to 'near fly' from the summit down to the Games Park when we realised that a football match was taking place beneath us. Then schooldays were over.

School report card

Chapter 27.

An ill wind

Blow, blow, thou winter wind:
William Shakespeare: As You Like It

Saturday morning, 31st January 1953, dawned bitterly cold. There had been a heavy shower of wet snow overnight, but an East wind was rising, freezing the blanket of snow, creating top-heavy trees and blizzard conditions on roads. First casualties were power and phone lines carrying massive ice loads; the cables and poles simply collapsed. By mid-morning Ballater was cut off; fallen trees had rendered roads and railway lines impassable. Structural damage became evident as unremitting gales grew in intensity. The station's platform canopy shattered and fences disappeared. The front window of John Smith's cycle shop blew in and promptly blew out the side wall of the building. Roofs blew off out-buildings, slates peeling off like so many pigeons breaking out of a wood; henhouses took, tumbling, to the fields and broken rabbit hutches freed tame rabbits to interbreed with the wild for generations to come. But that night we settled down, once everyone was safely home with his or her own story of the day, to an evening of log fires and candles, and to 'lie quiet till the storm blew by'.

Next morning was calm and sunny, and the deep deep snow hid much of the damage. I remember the tame and brilliant-coloured waxwing birds that covered the cotoneaster hedges in Queens Road feasting on the red berries. The old folk declared that the flocks had been blown across from Scandinavia by the gale.

It was some time before proper assessments of the damage could be made. A ferry had been lost on the Scotland-Belfast run; large areas of the English East coast were under water, but on Deeside we simply lost our trees. For a valley that had sacrificed 500,000 tons of timber to the war effort a scarce eight years earlier, to lose hundreds of thousands of mature trees to a gale in one day was truly devastating.

In normal timber harvesting operations, the hillside involved shows the scars till replanting or natural regeneration takes over, but the forests that have suffered from extensive wind blow have the added embarrassment of a sea of upturned

Clearing the drive to Tillypronie House

root systems. That mix of holes and towering plates of stone, clay and stumps makes for difficult and dangerous extraction with a finite two years to complete the work before dry weather and insects render the trees valueless.

The task of salvaging that mighty windfall started at once, with priority given to opening roads. The immense ornamental spruce trees that lined many estate drives were simply too big to handle with the equipment immediately available, so the expeditious answer was to cut out the section blocking the road, drag the log to one side and attack the next tree.

Encouraged by Government aid to what were indeed disaster areas, whole new sawmills were set up. Evans of Widnes took over an area close to the golf course, latterly WWII soldiers' stables and now the Caravan Site. Like the Canadians before them, Evans brought in modern equipment with hitherto unknown band saws. Once set up, they started hiring men.

During the war, everything was highly organised and Canadians, Newfoundlanders, military and timber control personnel were living and working under military discipline and the constraints of war-time controls. Accordingly, a police sergeant and one constable, with the support of the Royal Military Police, sufficed to keep the peace.

The year 1953 was quite different; the local shortage of labour pushed up wages and attracted that floating pool of workers that follows the big money, not necessarily men skilled in timber handling. They came from the hydro-electric dams and tunnels; from long-distance lorry driving; they came from the coal mines; they came from the whaling fleet and trawlers; they came from building sites and they came from Ireland.

At that time, some East European displaced people that had resisted repatriation to a now Communist state were wandering, stateless and paperless, picking up dangerous work in hydro tunnels until officialdom loomed near, then moving again. A party of those 'Poles', 'Lithuanians', 'Czechs', never Germans, started work in a side glen.

In the 1950s National Service faced almost all young men of 18 years. That was unless they were farmers, miners, teachers or gained deferment to complete apprenticeships. The 1953 gale and the chaos it brought came as a Godsend to many draft dodgers, who came with new identities, mainly to work as self-employed sub-contractors and ride out the draft in some remote glen.

In the village, most men with secure jobs stayed put in the knowledge that that latest boom would have a very finite life. School-leavers never had it so good, starting in the brand-new saw mill at £15 per week. A bus driver set himself up as a haulier with a pre-war Leyland Beaver truck. A chef from the Invercauld Hotel became a sawmiller after 20 minutes' tuition. The waste was unbelievable; at 4pm every afternoon, a whistle would blow and this was the signal for half the housewives in Ballater to rush down to the sawmill with an assortment of carts, prams and washing baskets to share in the hand-out of wood offcuts.

All that free firewood spawned a home-made saw bench in every back yard. Basically, they were made up of a circular saw coupled to an engine which could be of any description, from a single cylinder stationary engine of agricultural origin to a motor-cycle engine (these tended to heat up in the absence of cooling air flow) and more commonly an old car engine complete with radiator. The drive was either by chain or flat belt. The common factor was the complete lack of guards and disregard for safety. Why there were no reportable injuries I will never know, as these engines ran at high speed and the saw blades snaked alarmingly.

Col Milne's two International trucks came out of retirement to help feed that mill, and a fish-lorry driver who, realising that traffic police on the A1 were losing patience with him, and that a sabbatical on Deeside would be a good idea, was appointed driver of the 'big' International.

Charlie's saw bench

In that wild world of the Coronation year, I left school and found holiday work in a wind-flattened wood high above Balmoral Castle.

The trees were first cut off the upturned roots; freed of the weight of the tree, the root system would flap back into place. Next, the branches were hacked off with an axe and the top of the tree sliced off when a diameter of five inches was reached. At that stage a tractor, in this case a Fordson Major powered by a Perkins P6 diesel engine and fitted with a Hesford winch, collected several trimmed trees and dragged them out of the wood and down to a rough track. More wood-cutters cross-cut the 50-foot trees into 8- and 12-foot logs. Another tractor and four-wheeled cart were hand loaded with the logs, and it made a steep descent to the roadside.

At the roadside waited the Crossley. That was an ex-RAF petrol-engined, four-wheel-drive truck that had spent the war towing trailers loaded with bombs out across the tarmac to Halifax heavy bombers on an East Anglian aerodrome. The Crossley had reached Deeside via the war surplus sales at Ruddington and had spent time working on estates before just happening to be in the right place at the right time when the windblow had suddenly put heavy haulage at a premium.

The Crossley was designed as a military 3-ton tractor, but the loads of logs we crawled out of the woods with used to weigh over 12 tons on the Evans saw mill weighbridge in Ballater. The truck used to haul four loads a day and it was also our transport home on the last load. Four of us used to squeeze into the high cab. With only two seats, the smallest—I and the contractor's son—had to sit on the engine cover.

The great four-cylinder engine was very heavy on fuel and for this reason the driver would throw it out of gear on any down-hill slope. From Coilacriech Inn, the trick was to free-wheel all the way to Bridge of Gairn, and, if 60 mph had been achieved by the Winny Turn, the truck would have enough momentum to carry it up to the gates of Craigendarroch Hotel and thence down the Darroch into Ballater.

That was a great saving of fuel but in retrospect a totally unacceptable risk; the vehicle was in effect out of control for four miles, the primitive brakes could never have held the truck had anything gone wrong and of course it was illegal to coast at all.

On other days, the Crossley failed to return for the last load and the old Austin truck of dairy days would appear as transport. We certainly felt safer running back to Ballater in it.

Between its milk-cart days and its then function as a contractor's hack, the old Austin had been bought by house painters. The principal was close to retiring, but his son had returned from being a wireless operator in the RAF and the leasing of a little shop and investing in transport was his contribution to modernity in the family business.

The summer of 1953 steamed on; Deeside was back in boom times, sawmills worked all hours and the Deeside railway carried the sawn timber to markets in the South and pit props to the still-buoyant coal mines. All winter the clear-up continued; the most accessible trees had been salvaged and the fortunes that were to be made had been made. By 1954 the pace of work was in decline; a hot summer had reduced the value of the fallen trees through advancing decay and the ever-increasing cost of recovering the trees lying in less-accessible woods. The one exception was the European larch, which proved much more resistant to the weather and bugs, and it was inherently more valuable. The work carried on into 1955: by that time, most of the larger mills had closed, been dismantled, and gone.

The Crossley

Chapter 28.

Technical studies

A man must serve his time to every trade:
George Gordon, Lord Byron:
English Bards and Scotch Reviewers

School was left behind in June 53. I had four weeks' holiday before starting my pre-apprenticeship course at Aberdeen Trades College in August. Going to 'Trades School' in Aberdeen meant catching the 7am train from Ballater each morning. There were few passengers boarding there and it was most unusual to see anyone at Cambus o' May. A potential joiner awaited the train at Dinnet and at Aboyne my carriage compartment filled up with more 'Trades School' students, escapees from the dreaded alternative: three years of Classics at Banchory Academy. Our fellow-travellers were becoming more interesting; girls began filling up the adjacent compartment en route to Webster's Secretarial College.

As the steam engine puffed us away from the Dee Valley to Dess Station and the detour that would take us to Lumphanan, Torphins and Glassel before rejoining the Valley at Banchory, we had crowds of secondary scholars boarding on their way to Banchory Academy. After Banchory station, the train was definitely quieter but filled up again with the commuters getting on at Crathes, Park and more especially Culter.

Culter was an interesting station to approach because as you passed the paper mills there was a funny little engine shunting wagons in and out of the mill on to the main line to join up with goods trains. By my time, there was only the Cults station left to stop at but in pre-war days there had been a host of suburban halts as you neared Aberdeen Joint Station.

That station did have a very pervasive smell of fish. Whole trains of fish hurried South each day, and the granite-cobbled roads between fish houses and station trapped the 'fish bree' to give Guild Street its unique odour. We crossed the Green, with its open-air market on Fridays, went through Correction Wynd into the thronging crowds on George Street, a George Street that still rattled with old open-ended trams and boasted Isaac Benzies's department store and the Rubber Shop. We took a short cut into John Street that passed a rag-and-bone merchant's premises, and, judging from the smell, he must have majored in bones.

Then we were at the Trades College. Aberdeen Trades College trained youngsters for one year to give them grounding in engineering or construction before starting their apprenticeships. The college Principal was a Mr Cunningham, known to all the students as 'Sly Bacon.'

The section that I enrolled in taught boys the basics of general engineering for six months. We would then concentrate on our preferred subjects for the second six months. We also studied applied maths, technical drawing and current affairs and were given an awareness of local government.

Jim Leslie was the motor engineering instructor; his strong subject was the theory of motor-car steering systems. Jim was always lamenting the then new systems of independent front suspensions that upset all his theories and wore out tyres. He ruled an extensive workshop with a complete Leyland Lynx truck chassis and a car he had been building since the end of the war.

A Mr MacDonald taught us electrics and we learnt how to solder and wire up lights. When he discovered that I came from Ballater, he told me that he had served part of his apprenticeship there, wiring the village for electricity from a large engine-driven generator at the locally known power station. He then asked me if I knew certain girls there whom he named. The names didn't ring bells with me, and that night I asked my mother if she knew about whom he had been speaking. It turned out that Mr MacDonald had been speaking of maiden names of his youth but these 'girls' had long since married and were now grandmothers. I hadn't the heart to tell him.

The winter passed and we got used to the long days of early, cold mornings and dark winter return journeys. Friday nights were a release and the Webster Secretarial girls talked with us on the train home and we planned our Saturday nights. Saturday-night dances were a strange mixture of ritual and demand. In Upper Deeside at that time, there would be an 'in place' to go and in 1954 it was the British Legion Victory Club wooden building or 'The Hut' as we knew it, in Ballater.

Young folk came from far and near to those dances and, because of the upsurge in forestry activity courtesy of the '53 Great Gale, Ballater was in the midst of a boom. Indeed it became a real frontier town on Saturday nights; many of the migrant woodcutters descended on Ballater's two pubs and when closing time came at 10pm they swelled the crowds going to the dance.

The girls had already been there since 9pm., partnering each other to the Gay Birds dance band that was taking this opportunity to practise the latest hits before the real crowd came in with the pub closing time. At 10pm, the trickle of patrons had swollen to a torrent all anxious to spend the half-crown that would gain them access to the Promised Land.

You entered the building, paid the entry fee over to the eager British Legion members, turned left along a passage then right into the dance-hall. The band was on the stage on your right; it really didn't matter too much who was playing. Ballater was the place to be that night and being there was all that mattered.

Between dances, the girls retreated to the far side of the hall, forming a line-up the length of the dance floor, while the men crowded the opposite side of the room. When the next dance was announced, there was a mad rush over the floor to claim your partner of choice.

At the top of the hall, a small door led off to an ante-room that served tea and soft drinks, sausage rolls and chocolate biscuits. There could be found the non-dancing fraternity, coolly swigging beer from screw-top bottles that shared their tables with pints of whisky. There the intelligentsia sat concluding the debates initiated earlier in the Tink Bar.

All that activity came to a sudden end at the witching hour of midnight. The band had announced the last waltz, girls were held in the arms of their beaux, and everyone had to be off the premises, waiting only for a few bars of 'God save the Queen'.

Outside all was a mêlée; taxis were waiting to transport dancers' home to exotic places like Towie, Tarland, Logie Coldstone and Aboyne, and in the Station Square a bus wanted to depart for Crathie and all points west.

All that hindered that logistical movement was the path of true love that refused to give up partners who lived at the opposite ends of the Dee Valley. Gradually, dishevelled lovers appeared from behind buildings, out of bushes and the back seats of other people's cars to climb reluctantly aboard transport to another celibate week.

Chapter 29.

Specialist in the Unusual

Good engineers are so scarce, that one must bear with their humours:
Lord Galway, Massue de Ruvigny:
Dispatch from Spain, 1704

It was back to college Monday morning, back to the train journey, little dreaming how short a time the Deeside Line had left. But those Monday mornings it was business as usual: the railway staff we had got to know were friendly easy-going folk, with, as they thought, a strong union and a job for life. That didn't preclude risking all through back-dating racehorse winning bets by taking advantage of railway mail franking that timed half-hour intervals, which was a time difference in which you could learn the winner by radio and post your winning bet at the next station within the half-hour. It must be said that the bets and winnings were kept modest to avoid suspicion.

It was halfway through March '54, and my sixteenth birthday. Although the college course ran till June, all students were free to leave after their sixteenth birthday if they had an apprenticeship to go to.

My fascination with machinery started with my earliest memories of army trucks and Bren-gun carriers sharing Ballater streets with Indian Army mule trains and Canadian Forestry Corps timber trucks in war-time Ballater.

Strangely enough, my last year at Ballater School had coincided with a second boom that had followed the Great Gale of 31st. January 1953. In the space of two hours, 5,000,000 trees were uprooted in the North-East of Scotland. Many, many acres of Deeside forestry that survived the 500,000 tons of war-effort felling, were blown down in a 100mph East wind.

That unexpected windfall attracted an influx of entrepreneurs. Among the new-comers to that trade was a Royal Engineer, a former captain, Peter Mckenzie Kaye. Peter Kaye was a tall, lean, Yorkshire man from Leeds with a heavy RAF-type moustache and at 32 years of age, already quite bald. I persuaded my mother to speak to him on my behalf and we were invited down to Glascorrie, his parents' home, for a chat.

Glascorrie, two miles east of Ballater on the South Deeside road, was served by the local bus company, but, not being on the main North Deeside route, was serviced by the older buses of the fleet. Saturday afternoon we boarded a Strachan's pre-war Albion bus and rattled down to Glascorrie road end. The grounds around the house were littered with ex-army trucks in all states of disrepair. Peter's main business was converting army trucks into forestry cranes. That day it was a very exciting place to be.

We were met and ushered into the front room. Peter was a man of great charm and we soon felt at ease. He asked me questions about lathe and machine work, about the college and my School Leaving qualifications. He then outlined his own operations, acknowledging that the current demand for cranes would dry up as the backlog of timber was cleared, but that he hoped to carry on in general engineering and hinted that there could be an involvement with racing-car tuning.

The interview was over: could I start first week in April? I had got my first job.

American Willys Jeep

That first Monday, I got on my bike and pedalled off to Glascorrie. Close to the house was a tiny, tiny garage; inside was the chassis of a Willys Jeep, obviously in the process of rebuild, complete with wheels and fresh aluminium paint. A bench with a vice occupied the end of the shed and shiny, chrome socket keys were lined up on the sill of the only small, cobwebbed window.

My first workshop

As I took all of that in, a small Austin Seven rattled by and Peter's only other employee appeared. I knew him by sight and my grandmother's nickname 'Parafinella', her amalgam of Paterson and the smell of paraffin that mechanics used to clean oil off their hands. Soon afterwards Peter came striding out of the woods from his own little house called appropriately enough 'Woodlands'.

The immediate job was quite ambitious. Large silver spruce trees that had been blown down in the grounds of Birkhall House had proved too heavy for the tackle of the contractor landed with the job of removing them and he had called on Peter Kaye to assist. Peter had responded to that challenge with a short-wheelbase ex-army Canadian-built Chevrolet truck equipped with a Kaye-fitted American Garwood winch.

That machine had successfully winched several large trees out. The next tree was much heavier and winching only pulled the truck backwards to the load. Peter then chained the front of the truck to a standing tree and, so locked, started to winch again. This time the mighty tree did start to creep up the slope, but jammed itself behind a stump. As Peter continued to pull, there was a sudden crack and the driving chain flew off the winch. On examination, it was found that the truck, chained as it was at the front, and unable to move the jammed log, had neatly kinked the chassis frame. No longer in line, the chain had sprung off.

With a bent chassis, the truck was useless. It had been driven home like a camel all humped up in the middle and now it was my first job to fit a replacement chassis frame that Peter had found in an ex-army dump near Leeds.

At lunch time, I examined the other vehicles scattered about. The half-rebuilt Jeep was Peter's personal transport; he could never give up his army background. There was a second, later model, Canadian Chevrolet truck in the process of restoration; then another Jeep-like vehicle, only larger. I asked Parafinella what it was and I thought he said it was Dutch. He talked with a lisp and I later discovered it was a Dodge. A third Chevrolet lay without a driver's cab farther away.

Day two was more eventful. Peter's father still worked Glascorrie as a small-holding and that day the Dept. of Agriculture contractor had appeared with a crawler tractor and plough and was reseeding the steep fields above the house.

Caterpillar D2 ploughing

Peter was fascinated by that tractor and explained to me that the yellow D2 was a genuine American-built Caterpillar, and so I learnt then that not all crawler tractors were Caterpillars. We left the Caterpillar to the ploughing and continued with our Chevrolet. The new chassis was already sitting on its wheels and the next job was to lift in the engine. As there was not a Kaye crane complete, Peter had us rig up three poles tied together to form a set of sheer-legs. With that rig, we used a block and tackle to hoist the engine high enough for us to push our chassis underneath and then to lower the engine into place. However, as we gave a last tug on the chain to lift the engine over some obstacle, one of the poles of our sheer-legs broke and the engine fell into the chassis, but not before Parafinella and I had to jump for our lives.

Everybody got angry. Peter was angry because the engine was damaged. Parafinella was angry to start with because he had almost been killed and then because he had an argument about back pay, and suddenly he was gone, his Austin Seven jingling furiously up the hill. At that point, Peter took me into his mother's kitchen and we all had cocoa and cake. I got the impression that he was relieved Parafinella had gone, and I needed a lot less wages anyway.

Somehow we managed to complete the rest of the work together and it was very satisfying to see the truck totally rebuilt, refitted with its crane and sold.

Canadian Chevrolet

That crane was bought by A. & M. Carmichael & Co., of Edinburgh. That company, along with many other civil engineering contractors, was deeply involved in the construction of the North of Scotland Hydro-Electric Board's dams and tunnels throughout the Highlands. However, that crane was destined to load timber in the Glen of Dye, where Carmichael had a large logging camp. Most of their labour came over from Donegal, and the blown timber gave work to both men and trucks and provided a source of timber for their shuttering work on the mass concrete dams.

The next crane order came from the Forestry Commission. Peter had sought out a late-model Canadian Chevrolet with what was known as a Desert Pattern cab, with windows that tilted back from the top to minimise glare, very much like modern naval wheelhouse practice. That truck also had heavy-duty axles and the Garwood winch. Peter opted to farm out the welding to a firm of engineers in Stonehaven, and the bare chassis and cab were duly delivered there, where the crane part of the truck was fabricated and fixed to the chassis.

While that work was being done, Peter took the opportunity to travel South by rail to Ruddington, where, nine years after the end of the war, surplus vehicles were still being auctioned. Before he left, he instructed me to decarbonise the engine of the Jeep-like Dodge. That entailed removing the cylinder head, taking out the valves, cleaning the carbon deposits off the pistons, cylinder head and valves. After having the valves refaced at Strachan's Garage, I ground in the valve seats, and then reassembled the motor.

On my own, it took the best part of that week. The Jeep had to first be pushed out of the little shed. I was not strong enough to push the Dodge, but, once I had removed the cylinder head, I was able to crank the engine in low gear and so wind the truck inside the shed door. It was too long to get right inside, so I had to crank the Dodge out every night to get the shed locked up.

By experimenting with the gear handle, I discovered that, other than in low gear and reverse, I was unable to crank the engine. This taught me more about gear ratios than all the text books and colleges put together.

American Dodge

By Friday, the Dodge was reassembled and running. It was a great incentive for a 16-year-old to complete the work just to be able to get to drive this powerful vehicle about the farm grounds.

Peter was nowhere to be seen when I arrived at Glascorrie on the Monday morning but standing in the yard, coupled together with a short veebar, were two trucks. They had the same Desert Pattern cabs as the Canadian Chevrolet being prepared for the Forestry Commission, but embossed on the metal-work around the radiator grille was the legend 'Canadian Ford'. Both were of very short wheelbase and were kitted out as water tankers; beyond that, both were covered in preservation grease and were brand new.

Peter had single-handedly driven one towing the other all the way from Ruddington, Yorkshire. The legality of the operation occupied a grey area of transport law. Peter had taken the precaution of displaying trade plates, which gave him some immunity from traffic police, but he relied principally on wearing fresh white overalls and confusing the over-zealous with his best British Army Officer accent when interrogated.

Anyway, the trucks were home; the water tanks were removed, fitted with wheels and immediately sold to farms. One truck was temporarily cannibalised for spares while the other was fitted with a swinging timber bolster and trailer to transport 30-foot-long logs from Tillypronie Estate down into Dinnet station to be transferred to railway wagons. Peter Kaye retained ownership of that truck and trailer although it was hired out to and operated by another English company by the improbable name of Enthistle and Bacon. That company had been drafted in to salvage the wind-blown timber on Lord Astor's Tillypronie Estate, and this hire arrangement marked the start of Peter Kaye's career in contracting.

The sale of the Chevrolet crane to the Forestry Commision was running into trouble. The truck was back at Glascorrie being prepared for delivery when word came that the Forestry Commision's workshop foreman was refusing to accept an ex-army truck fitted with an 18-foot crane, on safety grounds. Because it was a lifting device, and subject to statutory controls, Peter Kaye invited an inspection by a Chartered Insurance Engineer.

The engineer duly appeared, spent some time photographing the crane and studying a copy of Peter's engineering calculations. After receiving a mug of cocoa and a slice of cherry cake, plus a heaped basket of fresh garden vegetables from Peter's mother, the inspector declared that he was satisfied with the safety of our crane and signed an endorsement.

The Forestry Commission foreman was still making silly noises to head office, and Peter invited the office to send their foreman to Glascorrie to inspect the truck for himself. Several days later, the offending foreman and a mechanic arrived.

The mechanic inspected the vehicle and could find no fault, but still the foreman kept muttering about stability. 'Ok,' said Peter, 'jump in'. All three climbed into the cab, Peter driving, the mechanic sitting on the engine cover and the foreman in the passenger seat.

Immediately in front of Glascorrie farm house is a steep field that rises straight up to the South Deeside Road. Peter drove the crane into the field and started climbing; at the steepest part, he turned through 90 degrees and drove along the slope. Peter had turned left, ensuring that he was on the uphill side of the truck, but the Forestry Commission pair was in a far more exposed position. Even watching it was scary, but to have been in that cab must have been absolutely terrifying.

Peter turned the large four-wheel-drive down hill and out through the field gate. The two Forestry Commission men couldn't get out quickly enough. Not another word was spoken and they jumped into their van and sped off. Next morning, Peter got a phone call from Forestry Commission Head Office, Queen's Gate, Aberdeen. It said simply: 'Please deliver our crane without further delay'.

Our next project was a Studebaker Weasel. That was a small rubber-tracked machine, a bit like a Land Rover but it had a hull and could cope with soft, wet ground, deep snow, steep hills or float on water. Like the Willys Jeep, the Weasel was a product of WWII American Army engineering innovation. That machine was being converted from army specifications to suit the needs of a Highland estate.

The client was the Earl of Airlie, who had ordered the Weasel for his Tulchan Lodge in upper Glen Isla. Traditionally, the work of bringing in the stags that the stalkers had culled was done with garrons, the sturdy Highland hill ponies, but now the Studebaker Weasel was going to help.

Studebaker Weasel

The work we did on the Weasel was mainly an engine overhaul and supplying and fitting a green canvas awning and seats to the cargo area. We also welded in a new steel floor. The Weasel was duly loaded on a haulier's Leyland Beaver and departed for steepest Perthshire.

After only a few weeks, it was reported that the Weasel tracks were giving trouble. Peter ordered new bogeys and rubber tracks and early one September morning we loaded tools and spares into the Jeep and set off over the Devil's Elbow to Glen Isla. It was late September and quite frosty that morning and really cold at high speed in the open Jeep.

Tulchan was a Victorian shooting lodge set at the junction of Glen Brighty with Glen Isla at an altitude of 1401 feet, sheltered from the winter winds by a mature

Upper Glenisla

Earl of Airlie's Tulchan Lodge

fir wood. The hills closed it in with steep, green slopes and this secluded spot was as far into the high hills as the Victorians could possibly have built.

We found our Weasel with faulty feet behind the lodge and so started replacing the running gear with the help of the two stalkers. The problem had been caused by the rubber components having perished during their eight-year storage since coming out of army use. That weakness had not showed up until the strenuous work on the hills.

My memories of that day are of giant midges; the unwelcome attention of Labrador dogs; the welcome attention of inquisitive House guests, especially that year's debutantes, who seemed fascinated by Peter's moustache. The Earl of Airlie at that time was chairman of the North of Scotland Hydro-Electric Board and chairman of a major Scottish bank. Of course his son, Angus Ogilvie, went on to marry Princess Alexandra, daughter of the Duchess of Kent.

By late afternoon, the Weasel was reassembled and ready to test. Peter drove and a flurry of young girls, each a Lady in her own right, along with a pack of Labrador dogs, jumped in the back. Peter picked the steepest slopes to try out the machine and as it began to climb steeper and higher we were entertained by the squeals of Ladies and Honourables, and the further spectacle of dogs sliding backwards on the steel floor of the Weasel, all four feet desperately trying to arrest their eviction.

The test drive completed to Peter's satisfaction and the departure of dishevelled debutantes, we collected up our tools and spares. The Head Stalker then said. 'The Laird wants you to have your supper in the bothy before you go'. So supper it was. The stalkers grew their own cabbage and potatoes and served them up in venison stew, followed up by strawberries and cream sent over from the Lodge. Along with the dessert came a bottle of whisky with the Laird's compliments.

The two stalkers helped us finish that bottle before we roared back over the Elbow to Braemar, then home in the open Jeep. There were then more cranes to build; one went to Ross-shire, another to Durris, and finally, the Dodge was fitted up with a short jib to load the railway wagons at Dinnet Station with the ever-increasing loads of timber coming out of Tilliepronie Estate.

Among the strangers that were attracted by the wind blow to Deeside was a New Zealander. He came as a tourist, travelling pillion seat on his friend's Matchless motor-cycle, and decided to stay and work in the woods. He was singularly successful, applying colonial skills that wider horizons had developed to the opportunities on hand, and soon he was looking for two

Devil's Elbow on A93

cranes. He saw how Peter Kaye travelled down to Ruddington sales and drove the vehicles North and decided that he could do the same. The New Zealander bought two Canadian Fords at the sale, got as far as Scotch Corner, then phoned for Peter to get the trucks home.

Peter was getting more and more involved with the contracting side of the timber business. Most of the work was coming from the English company working at Tillypronie and right then his need was crawler tractors to keep the timber extraction going through the wet winter ahead. The New Zealander's plea for help couldn't have come at a better time. Peter made a deal with him to recover his trucks for a sum of money that would handsomely finance his next trip south in search of tractors.

A week later, Peter and a contractor friend drove into Glascorrie. Their convoy consisted of another Canadian Ford with steel body that Peter had bought towing one of the New Zealander's Fords. Peter's truck had a Caterpillar 22 crawler tractor in the body, while the towed Ford was festooned with winches and skid chains. The New Zealander's second Ford truck was pulling a low-load trailer on which was sitting a large orange-painted diesel Cletrac crawler.

The New Zealander had got his trucks home and Peter had his crawler tractors all in one momentous operation. That convoy had negotiated the Devil's Elbow at night and in snow. More than that, the second Ford had started to suffer from fuel starvation and Peter had reversed, chained the four vehicles together and one Ford's V-8 engine had pulled the

The Cletrac

whole train round the notorious Z-bend and on over the hill; total train weight was well in excess of 30 tons. Peter was not seen for two days after that.

The crawlers duly went to work at Tilliepronie and the call went out for more crawlers as demand for their special duties grew. An island on the Loch of Aboyne was covered in blown pine trees but no-one could reach them with ordinary, wheeled, tractors.

Peter had heard of an ex-Forestry Commission Caterpillar R2 with wide soft-ground tracks. We duly set off and collected that machine, hauled it to the loch, and, talk about walking on water, Peter drove the machine over the reed beds on to the island.

We then started pulling the logs off the island. Everything went well at first, but Peter ventured into the water and floated the trees behind him; this way he could pull twice as many each trip. After a few trips, the soft mud had the R2 sinking deeper and deeper till suddenly the fan started splashing in the water, the magneto got soaked and the engine stopped at a deep hole. Peter had to send for a tractor with a heavy-duty winch to drag the drowned R2 out to dry land. Next day, we went back and finished the job without wading in the loch.

For the rest of the winter of 1954/55, I spent half my time repairing trucks and the rest driving the large orange Cletrac in the woods. One memorable night I drove the Cletrac four miles over snow bound roads between woods. There was a need for a larger truck, so Peter bought a pre-war ex-fish trade Leyland Beaver that had been burnt and had no cab. Peter got the local joiners to build a rudimentary cab with plywood. There was no back to the cab or doors, just a shed on wheels. That monster was set to hauling trees into Dinnet Station.

All went well until the local policeman, smarting over many run-ins with Peter Kaye where he had come off second best, pounced on the Beaver. Peter and he argued about that cab, but the bobby's knowledge of Construction and

Use Regulations was no match for Peter's silver tongue. Next day, a whole posse of police stood in the road at Dinnet. They included the local bobby, a contingent from the Traffic Police with a Wolseley patrol car and the Inspector from Aboyne Police Station. Still no fault could be found with the mechanical condition of the Beaver, but an eagle-eyed traffic officer noticed that our bold Peter was carting timber on trade plates, which covered only 'testing' or transporting empty vehicles from A to B. That transgression sounded the end for our Beaver.

Peter could see that the Tillypronie work was coming to an end; all the timber that could economically be salvaged had been extracted although work there continued into 1955; by late December 1954 Peter was looking ahead.

Chapter 30.

A far cry to Loch Awe

Is fad an eubh o Loch Obha [Far's the cry from Loch Awe]
Is cobhair o Chlann 0 Duibhne [and help from the race of O'Duibne]:
Clan Campbell saying

The above, oft mistaken for a Campbell boast, was in fact a lamentation. It arose; legend has it, when hard pressed by the Gordons at Allt Chuailleachain in Glenlivet in their 1594 battle. There they first encountered cannon, *mathair nam musgaid* [the muskets' mother] to the West Highlanders.

It was still a far cry from the North-east to Argyll in my young days, as my account of the following expedition will demonstrate.

At that time, the Caledonian Propping Company was a large concern that specialised in providing pit props for the coal mines. It was advertising for contractors to cut and extract large quantities of mining timber in Argyll. Peter McKenzie Kaye replied, and was invited to Oban for a meeting on the 2nd January 1955. Transport for the trip was a problem. Oban in January and a 400-mile round trip were not for Peter's open Jeep. His solution, however, was not exactly the last word in luxury travel. The New Zealander for whom Peter had recovered the trucks owned an eight hp Ford van and this was to be our transport to Oban.

Fifty years ago, Scotland suffered a sad lack of roads to link the East and West Coasts, and today the problem has still to be addressed. Mid-winter 1955, the problem was compounded by the road South from Braemar being almost permanently closed, blocked by snow. The ski-ing activity on 'Glenshee' and that impetus to keep the road open were still ten years away.

The next 'short cut' over the Cairn o' Mount was also closed, so in the winter darkness we drove over the Slug Road to Stonehaven and turned South for Perth and distant Argyll. The Aberdeen road South ran through all the small towns, and by the time we reached Perth it was just waking up. There we got out of the little van, frozen with cold and stiff from sitting, drank a flask of tea, and left an icy Perth on the Crieff road.

After Comrie and St. Fillans, we drove west along Loch Earn. High above the road a hydro-electric scheme tunnel was being driven by Mitchell Construction of Peterborough. Later that year, their tunnel tigers set a new world tunnelling record there of 557 feet of 8.5 feet width in hard rock in the seven days from 20th to 27th. October 1955. As we drove along the loch side, we could see the spoil from the tunnel tipped along the roadside, to be later dozed into the water's edge, considerably widening and straightening the twisty road we used that morning. The tragedy for Scotland is that the loch side improvements stopped with the excavations from the scheme, barely half way along the loch, never to be completed 50 years on. Steep Glen Ogle sorely tested the little van; Crianlarich was a spaghetti junction of railway lines disappearing into misty hillsides. At Tyndrum, we saw a sign for Glen Coe then we turned left for Dalmally. Loch Awe appeared with an old castle on an island. The road literally hung above the water at the Pass of Brander. Later hydro-electric schemes hollowed out Ben Cruachan and transformed that section of the road.

We were running near the meeting time and Peter managed to get up more speed on this downhill rush to sea level at Loch Etive. Visibility had dropped with a real West Coast mist allowing view of only the road and ghostly, leafless, roadside trees. Peter had to slow the little van for the 30mph limits approaching Connel Ferry, then, suddenly, out of the mist and immediately above us were the massive girders of Connel Bridge. When completed in 1903, that bridge with its span of 690 feet was second only to the Forth Rail Bridge. The image of its ghostly, sudden appearance that morning has stayed with me ever since. We drove into Oban, quite a large town of tall sea-front hotels, harbours, water and seagulls, but surreally a ghost town, a town with no people, on January 2nd 1955 at 12 noon. Oban was still sleeping off the effects of Hogmanay 1954. No shops were open, hotels were closed, pubs were shut, and the railway station was deserted.

Worse was to follow; four representatives of the Caledonian Propping Company arrived on time, packed in an Austin car. They spoke with Peter and he came over and asked me to stay and look after the Ford van as there was no room for me in the Austin, and that the woods to be viewed were 30 miles away on an island. Resigned to my fate in the ghost town, I opened my piece bag and slowly ate sandwiches and buns.

I explored Oban in the gathering misty gloom of a mid-winter afternoon, remembering landmarks that would take on a very different aspect on my next visit ten years later in the bustle and colour of the summer holiday season.

It was quite dark before Peter returned from his island trip. He took leave of his Caledonian Propping pals, started up the little Ford, and then said the job was not for us.

The morning's journey was an adventure of travel and new places, but on the return I tried to sleep as much as one can sleep in a small van with two transverse springs, travelling at high speed on endlessly twisting roads. Eventually we arrived at Perth, then, just north of the town, our lights, poor at the best of times, started to dim. We both realised that the little 6-volt dynamo had given up charging.

The nearest Ford dealers were Mungall's of Forfar, and at 10pm we reached them with only side lamps left. Mercifully, the stores were still open, as the workshops were on late shift, and we managed to buy a set of dynamo brushes; fitting took another half-hour, but that solved the problem. Forfar was on the main trunk road south then and boasted an all-night transport café. We drove there, got refreshed, and carried on home to Ballater. The whole trip had taken from 5am on the 2nd January till 2am 3rd January. Such was life with one Peter Mckenzie Kaye.

Next day was back to work with crawler tractors and cranes; the hand-made cabbed Beaver was replaced by a five-ton Austin of fair age. Those Austins had a great engine but a weak chassis frame, and this one was no exception. While the Chevrolet truck had kinked its chassis upwards, like a camel, this Austin's chassis had kinked downwards and sagged like an old horse.

As 1955 wore on through Easter, the gale-blown timber was drying up rapidly and my Cletrac tractor and the Caterpillar R2 were sent to Dufftown to recover trees from some inaccessible hill that nobody else would touch. I stayed at base, increasingly involved with farmers' tractors and repairs.

One day Peter came and told me that he was moving to Edinburgh and that he had secured a contract to manufacture and fit thousands of metal links that were required on a civil engineering job. He had formed a company called Highland Engineering and was building a factory at Edinburgh, and would I come with him?

At that moment in time, I was earning £2 a week, that is the weeks Peter remembered, and with the Oban trip very fresh in my mind, I thought Edinburgh a very foreign country and said: 'No thanks'. For some time the local Riverside Garage had been urging me to come and work with them and later that day I confirmed that I could start on the Monday.

Peter McKenzie Kaye finished up his business in Ballater under a cloud; left for Edinburgh and some years later was deeply involved with the construction of the Forth Road Bridge. Following on from there, he initiated a hovercraft service on the Clyde; that venture was short-lived as the housewives of Largs objected to their washing taking off into orbit each time Peter's hovercraft turned in the bay, directing a lethal air stream at their washing lines.

Property and real-estate deals in Ulster, New Zealand, and in his native Leeds followed on after that and I last heard of him in the Channel Isles.

Chapter 31.

Spanners and the works

An apprentice for to bind:
> The Oxford Book of Ballads

It was a bright May morning when I started work at the Riverside Garage. In those days it was the first building as you entered Ballater, almost brand new, risen from the ashes of a pre-war garage that had burnt down early in the war.

There were two partners in the business, the senior of whom had been employed by the previous owner pre-war and who had ran the business from an old wooden shed throughout the busy but difficult war years. The junior partner was a war veteran, and that week he was on honeymoon in Jersey.

It was explained to me how to operate the petrol pumps, the cash register and how to write up the credit-sales ledger, and, although I had gone there to complete my apprenticeship as a motor engineer, I can honestly say that that was all the formal training I ever got.

Apart from the two partners, the staff of the Riverside Garage comprised one newly time-served apprentice awaiting National Service call-up, probably the reason that the partners were so keen for me to join, and another mechanic who was part and parcel of the deal that the partners bought from the previous owner.

That chap had returned from war service in the RAF and had worked at the old Riverside Garage pre-war. He used to recall the buzz in Ballater while the film of Queen Victoria's reign *Sixty Glorious Years* was shot at Balmoral in 1938, starring Dame Anna Neagle. All the cameramen and extras stayed in Ballater and every taxi in town was hired for the duration. Norman remembered the Deeside weather delaying the filming and the film crews passing the time gambling. He declared that he had never before or since seen so much money changing hands. ·

The Riverside Garage of Spring 1955 was a busy, successful enterprise. The River Dee was still a by-word in elite salmon fishing, the nearby Invercauld Hotel catered for the type of fisher that stayed for a month a time, employed

Anna Neagle at Balmoral 1938

one or more fishing ghillies, had his own chauffeur, and brought his wife with him, if not his whole family, to the delight of the local shopkeepers, who vied for this spring windfall.

The salmon fishers' Jaguars returned to Riverside each night to be put to bed with some unlikely bed-fellows. The carrier's lorry had to go in last because it left for Aberdeen at 6am every morning. The Fordson tractor with half its engine dismantled, the Co-op van getting new brake linings, a 1937 Rover 12, a 1934 Austin 12, the shoemaker's Vauxhall, the garage's 1936 Austin 10, the garage's 1934 Austin 16, the banker's Vauxhall, the big International truck of war-time timber work and lately of marathon use clearing up the '53 big-gale blown timber, and in the corner, covered in dust, the builder's Morris 10.

Outside was a wooden hut where the wet-acid wireless batteries were charged, now a store, and the old Austin 10 truck, last seen transporting woodcutters home from Balmoral's Ballochbuie Forest, now sitting on three wheels with a broken half-shaft.

The work at Riverside was gloriously varied. In the morning you could be repairing a puncture on a pre-war tractor and 2pm would find you setting the carburettor on the Laird's Bentley.

The junior partner returned from honeymoon and continued with his modernisation plans; a Land Rover was bought second-hand from a local estate to take over recovery work from the 1934 Austin 16. The Station Garage fell out with the Ambulance Service and the Riverside took over the Humber Pullman ambulance and the ambulance driver who had tended it from new. That meant that we had to take shifts of being on duty at nights, but as I was just 17 years old and I still had not passed my driving test, I did not qualify for ambulance driving.

In spite of not having a licence, I had been driving trucks, jeeps and heavy crawler tractors for the past year with Peter M Kaye. He had little concern for such details, and indeed on my 17th birthday in March I had bought the local tailor's Morris Minor, vintage 1933, that had spent the early war years transporting suits from Glasgow up over the Devil's Elbow to the Newfoundland and Canadian lumber camps to be sold to young lumberjacks keen to impress the local girls at the weekend dances.

In 1955, the Riverside Garage boasted two petrol pumps, Esso at 4 shillings and tuppence and Esso Extra at 4 shillings and sixpence per gallon. The junior partner had acquired a second-hand coat-of-arms from the grocer shop, and with great difficulty, attached it above the garage door, announcing to the world that the Riverside Garage had been awarded a Royal Warrant to repair the Royal tractors on Balmoral Estate. Thus equipped, we met the tourist summer.

Inside the garage, there was an office on one side and a car sales show-room on the other. The car sales never materialised and the space soon filled up with tyres. Behind the office was the washbed, and behind the show-room were a hydraulic ramp and service bay.

Beyond the washbed were long benches along the west wall, a light airy space with several large windows. The benches were equipped with vices, a vertical drill and a double-headed grinder. On the floor-space behind and parallel to the benches were two long pits, boarded over with strong removable planks. That was where most of the heavy repairs were done, replacing gearboxes and clutches. Those components were simply manhandled out of and into the vehicles by brute force.

On the rear wall of the building were windows on either side of another large door that was seldom used. A small welding booth was built beside that door in answer to my pleas for an electric-arc welder. I had learned to weld with Peter Kaye and found it impossible to work without one.

In the corner was a large square sawdust burner: this was a crowded, sought-after space in winter, a place we would retire to at 10am each day to eat butteries and drink tea out of flasks. The fuel for that heater came from the sawmill at the Station.

The task of collecting that sawdust was undertaken on the pretext of road-testing the latest tractor repair. I had just finished working on a large Case tractor when the senior boss told me to hitch up a trailer and fill it with sawdust, I drove to the sawmill, shovelled the trailer full and made my way back through the village.

The Case tractor

The big Case was proving a handful. There was no power steering in those days, and, to make matters worse, the clutch was operated by a hand lever instead of the usual pedal. When I got back to the garage, the drill was to reverse round the rear of the building as near as possible to the window beside the fire. This was easier said than done. This monster needed two hands for the steering, and the clutch demanded manual attention at the same time. The result was that the clutch went over centre, my steering fell behind and the rear of the trailer crashed through the window. The partners surveyed the damage, arranged for its speedy repair and the matter was never mentioned again.

Distractions took the shape of a long string of trekking ponies that carried girls past the garage every morning.

Tasks beyond the call of duty included picking up and disposing of a customer's dead Labrador dog that had been hit by a train. One early morning, a touring coach full of French school children stopped for fuel. The teachers made for our single toilet, but the teenagers crossed the road and attended to nature by the banks of the River Dee.

As summer wore on, we just became busier. Breakdowns were categorised; great priorities were given to AA and RAC members. The senior partner was highly skilled in evaluating strangers' ability to pay and set their credit ratings accordingly. We were instructed on a sliding scale from: 'Spare no expense' to: 'Get them past Aboyne', the logic being that a further breakdown would see the unfortunates at another garage.

August came, and I reminded the partners of their promise, made when I started, that they would allow me to continue with my one day-a-week Day Release classes at the Trades School through the winter. That announcement met with real resistance; it was easy to make promises in the slow month of May, but now it was high season and I could not be spared. I was suddenly indispensable. A compromise was struck. I could have my day off, but only on the firm understanding that I would make up my time by working four hours from 6pm to 10pm on Tuesdays and Thursdays one week, and Saturday afternoons and all day Sunday the alternate weeks. Oh! And for no extra money! I had no option but to agree. However, the Riverside was never the same after that, and my respect for the partners had gone.

My Tuesday and Thursday night sessions were worked with the junior partner: these were his nights on. The senior partner worked Mondays and Wednesdays, but he stayed in the office writing up the sales ledger and rarely ventured into the workshop. Riverside in those days never employed a clerkess, as in the senior partner's words: 'She would no sooner be trained than she would be married and gone'.

We got peace to concentrate on our work at nights; there were very little interruptions to serve petrol that we suffered from through the day. The junior partner became friendlier at night; we did have common interests in music, he played the fiddle and I had switched from the tyrannous classical piano lessons of my boyhood to the flexibility of playing popular and Scottish tunes on the accordion. From my 16th birthday I had been playing with my mother, along with another accordionist and drummer in the latest of the local bands.

That musical connection meant that the junior partner sometimes invited me to play with him at harvest homes, curlers' balls and other ceilidhs celebrated from Dinnet all up the valley to Braemar.

Playing at Invercauld Staff dance, December 1954

Although we were officially on duty till 10pm on our Tuesday/Thursday night shift, the junior partner would often stop at 9pm and start to reminiscence on his war service. The horrors of war affected everybody differently. The junior partner had been seriously ill with malaria in North Africa; this disease came back time and again. Listening as I did to his stories, and later seeing him suffer so, led me in later years to become convinced that the real junior partner died in the desert and that this man I knew had simply forced himself home like so many others. By November, I had to sit my driving test. Everybody agreed that it would be unwise to ask the test inspector to sit in my little Morris sans brakes, a passenger door that wouldn't shut properly, and broken seats, a legacy of the tailor's girth. The senior partner was keen for me to have a licence, for his own selfish reasons, and told me to take the Garage Austin 10 for the test.

The test went very well. I received the docket to exchange for a licence from the authorities and returned to the Riverside. I told the senior partner my good news as I removed the L-plates. 'I passed', I said. 'What other did you expect?', he replied.

The local policeman greeted the news with: 'Now keep it (the Morris) between the dykes'.

The year of 1955 came to an end and we enjoyed the only annual public holiday on 1st January.

I was settling into the garage routine; I much preferred to work on tractors and to weld rather than to service cars. The local forestry contractors were seeking me out for their repair work in the woods; this I enjoyed. The old Bedford, of coal delivery history, hurtled down the Darroch and ploughed into railings on the Darroch-Learg corner. It came to me at Riverside to build two new sections of rail and refit them. Fifty years later, we dug up the discarded, damaged and twisted railings while creating a drain for the new picnic area at Sluievannachie.

50 years on, James Cameron and the late Mike Sheridan inspect the remains, May 2005

The now Ballater Games Park used to be known as 'the cricket park' pre-war. So popular was the English game that in the park stood a heavy horse drawn granite roller complete with a rotten wooden frame and shafts. The Ballater Town Council laid claim to that wreck and decided that it should be fitted with a steel frame and then used to roll the new caravan park. That task was given to Riverside Garage and my electric-welding skills. Suffice to say that '50 years' on the roller is still used by Ballater Golf Course.

The Cricket Park roller

The Distillery at Crathie, home of Lochnagar Whisky, was being renovated: work included a 60-foot-high steel chimney. That three-foot diameter metal stack was stayed by four wire ropes attached to a clamp at 45 feet above ground. All summer that arrangement had worked well, but in colder weather the clamp loosened and slid down the chimney, resulting in the cables' becoming slack and allowing the chimney to move in the wind. Riverside Garage got the job of welding the offending clamp to the steel chimney, so fixing its position permanently. Guess who got the job to do?

The day picked for that operation was memorable for driving rain and sleet. Builders had put up a scaffold on three sides only of the stack. We set up our welder with long cables and I climbed up the 45 feet onto the scaffold. It was not a simple job I was wet through, terrified I was going to be electrocuted, and even refused a 'starting dram'.

Three sides fixed and only the bracket with no scaffolding left. I needed one hand to weld with and another to hold my mask. By that time I just wanted finished, so I, very foolishly as it turned out, discarded my mask, held on to the guy rope with one hand and welded without the protection of a mask.

I woke up in the middle of the night in agony. I was suffering from arc-welder flash.

With my new driving licence, I was getting quite adventuresome with the Morris Minor. We were much in demand as transport to local dances; first Dinnet, Crathie and Tarland. As Spring lengthened the days, our journeys' destinations reached into Donside. Weekend dance outings became more and more ambitious and reckless; first Corgarff, then Towie and finally Lonach via a lengthy stop at the legendary Boltenstone Inn.

That was a dance too far; after the last waltz, we set off for Kildrummy to party. We succeeded in passing most of the cars and taxis moving down Donside until, after passing a Rolls-Royce taxi, we were faced with a very tight corner.

Travelling far too fast to get round, the old Morris landed on its side and skidded to a halt in the middle of the road, in a shower of sparks and pools of oil. All the cars we had passed stopped, shining their lights on that unhappy scene.

We were shaken but unhurt. The Donsiders put the Morris on its wheels, push-started us and left us at the local garage. Long after midnight, Eddie Massie, proprietor, filled up the damaged radiator, put a couple of gallons of petrol in the fuel tank, and on being asked his professional opinion of whether the Morris would repair, memorably declared: 'Copydex and the welder and you will be all right'. The passengers that night, believe it or not, were a butcher and a baker!

To repair the Morris was not as simple as forecast. The ash framework of the body needed extensive repairs. We had run the engine dry before we reached Ballater and that burned one of the pistons. The little car was out of commission for most of the summer and I turned to a motor-cycle for mobility.

A confusing year was 1956. Anthony Eden with his French support invaded the Suez Canal zone to keep the canal out of Col Nasser of Egypt's control. The USA became angry and we were returned to petrol rationing just at a time that I was beginning to enjoy motoring. The rationing was most unfair; a woodcutter with a power saw was allocated more coupons than my little car, and the farmers had wads of them.

The apparent unfairness spawned crime and many a taxi ran dry in the middle of the night on the way home from dances, the unlocked fuel tank siphoned down by the less fortunate. The only perceptible plus point in all that was the relaxation of law that required learners to drive under the supervision of an experienced driver. Due to the fuel shortages, learners could study unsupervised, which meant that youngsters with cars could legally do what they had illegally been doing anyway.

Very soon, the Suez affair was having an effect on the country. Large pre-war cars fell in price; the baker with the yellow waistcoat came home from Aberdeen with an Austin 12, identical to his own, to be kept for spares: cost £40.

The local haulier, who had been in business since before the First World War, was taken over by a Banchory concern, and the big International truck of my childhood was towed away to be broken up. That started a clear-out in the garage and the builder's Morris 10 was towed outside and parked up beside the old Austin 10 truck. The next time I looked they had gone.

The years at Riverside slipped by, the work became easier as we became more experienced. Time came when my five-year apprenticeship, started with Peter Mckenzie Kaye and continued at Riverside, was over.

It took three paydays for the senior partner to acknowledge that I was no longer an apprentice and should now get journeyman's wages. Previous apprentices had been drafted straight into the forces immediately their time was served; my situation had no precedent.

The truth was that the Government was committed to stopping National Service all together, and the last batches of deferred call-ups were called in irregularly, as the Army could find places for them in its shrinking training facilities.

The next week's pay was paid at semi-skilled rate. That affront was all the more unacceptable as I held a City and Guild certificate in Technician's Work.

Some of our school friends, who had already finished their National Service, were called up as reservists in this emergency. Others were still serving their two years duty, resulting in a quieter Ballater on a Saturday night.

 I had registered for National Service at 18 years of age: my apprenticeship's deferred period was over. Now, as it hovered above me like the Sword of Damocles, there could be no long-term plans because sooner or later I had to go to National Service.

Chapter 32.

Warrants to warrant officers

This our bounden duty and service:
        The Book of Comon Prayer

During the First World War, a deposit of diatomite was worked on Dinnet Moor. The diatomite formed a white residue under the peat on the moor and in 1914 was greatly prized as an absorbent in the production of nitroglycerine. Mining production got under way; the moor was criss-crossed with light railways to convey the diatomite to a large sectional, curved-roofed, corrugated-iron shed. There the material was dried and packed before being dispatched South by goods train from Dinnet Station. The locals talked about the operation as 'the Kieselguhr', because that was the German name for the mineral.

After the war, the operation halted; several attempts since to evaluate the extent of the deposit and its potential have come to nothing. The rails were lifted and can yet be seen supporting the roofs of local farmers' sheds.

Enter one Lewis Gillies, very lately motor mechanic with John Milne the Carrier. That 1930s entrepreneur dismantled the old Kieselguhr shed and re-erected it in Victoria Road, Ballater, and set himself up there as motor engineer.

Luie Gillies ran a very successful business; after the war he obtained the Land Rover agency and was soon supplying all the sporting estates around with these four-wheel-drive vehicles.

Time went on and Luie Gillies decided to retire. His first employee, who had helped him dismantle and then erect his empire, and who had been with him ever since, apart from his WWII service in the RAF, took over the Victoria Garage. Those transactions coincided with my dissatisfaction with the Riverside Garage and I was quite happy to be head-hunted to join the new proprietor of the Victoria Garage.

There, standards of workmanship were definitely higher than was sought at Riverside. My new boss had been trained and worked on Rolls-Royce aircraft engines during his war service and I started to learn petrol engines all over again.

At Riverside, we had a Royal Warrant to repair estate tractors. At Victoria Garage, there were three Warrants to cover all the Royal Land Rovers and indeed Royal cars while they were at Balmoral.

August and September were hectic months. One morning the Royal Head Chauffeur from Balmoral came into the garage. He had a problem. A Royal Visit was planned for Orkney. Rather than risk the Daimlers on the island roads, it had been decided to use the Austin Sheerline. That car had a very low-slung exhaust system which would surely be damaged on Orkney. The Head Chauffeur had consulted the Austin Motor Company, and they had offered to redesign the whole exhaust pipe system, fabricate the parts, and dispatch them to Ballater. The Austin chief engineer would travel to supervise the work of fitting this raised pipework at the local garage.

The parts took some time to be made and arrived at Victoria Garage only the day before the Orkney Royal Visit. Panic stations: we worked all night. The modifications did not fit as simply as planned, but by 8am next morning the big Austin was ready and we were weary but happy as we awaited the Head Chauffeur. That gentleman duly arrived to announce that the trip was called off. Her Majesty was expecting another baby, he said, and she would visit Orkney another time.

January storm, 1960

Winter came and suddenly it was 1960. In the middle of January came a blizzard; it snowed for two days solid. Everything was snowed in. We took a whole day to dig out the forecourt of the garage and find the petrol pumps.

After that great feat, I retired to the First Class Bar at the station, started drinking brandy for some reason, snow-ploughed my way home, and woke up next morning to a monumental hangover and found my calling-up papers on the mat.

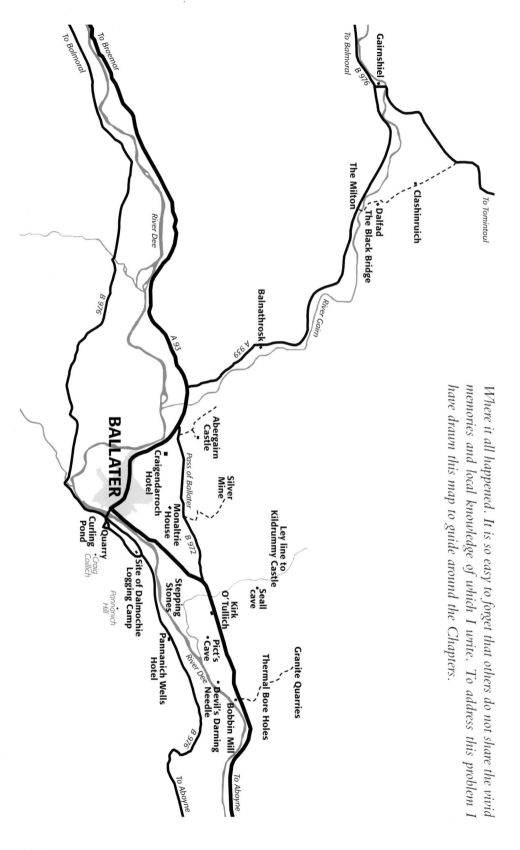

Where it all happened. It is so easy to forget that others do not share the vivid memories and local knowledge of which I write. To address this problem I have drawn this map to guide around the Chapters.

Appendix

The Ballater Historic Forestry Project Association

Re-creating the Newfoundland Logging Camp

A few Ballater folk that still remembered the war years and the members of Newfoundland Overseas Forestry Unit have formed the Ballater Historic Forestry Project Association to re-create part of the old logging camp as a museum, and as a tribute to the young men of Newfoundland.

The response has been amazing from both sides of the Atlantic: our Association has more than 80 members. The community council sponsored a feasibility study that agreed with our wishes and so opened the way for funding.

We drew up an initial programme of:

- Creating our own dedicated website to allow wider coverage of our aims. Visit www.ballaterforestry.org.uk

- Making a film: 'A Bygone Forest' telling the story and featuring Con Swyres, a logger who had actually stayed at Dalmochie, as the camp was known.

- Publishing a leaflet incorporating a guide map for the walk from the Tourist Office in Ballater's Old Station to the site of the camp.

- Finally, erecting three interpretation boards on the site of the log-cabin camp.

As I write, all these aims have been accomplished. We have also benefited from the Tourist Office's, allowing us to set up our film in the Old Station for viewing by visitors there. The next stage is to complete the funding to allow us actually to build log cabins again at Dalmochie.

The venture to date has been rewarding in many ways. Touchingly so, when veteran loggers give sincere thanks for not letting the story of their country's contribution to World War II be forgotten.

Index